LEARNING TO FLOAT

What My Conversations with Rob Bell Taught Me about Surviving Burnout and Creating a Life of Purpose & Joy

Dave Stradling

Cover Art: Justin Lamperski
Editing: Debbie Emmitt
Author Photo: Cassady K Photography
Book Layout Design: Megan McCullough

Published by: 30 Foot Salmon Publishing

ISBN: 979-8-9893561-2-6

Contents

Introduction

It was late 2017 when I officially burned out. I knew I'd been having trouble keeping my head above water for a while, but this was the moment I could no longer keep going.

The build-up had been years in the making. I'd started a church in 2012, and the emotional weight of carrying this church, along with my insecurities of needing external validation and wanting to meet every expectation, had left me exhausted. I was trying to be the person I thought others wanted me to be, instead of being true to who I was and the unique path I was being led down.

Thankfully, I've since recovered (albeit with a few scars) and have learned how to take better care of myself. The road to recovery hasn't been a straight path. Yet, here I am today, feeling more alive and more "me" than ever before.

Through my journey of burning out and learning how to create a new, sustainable life, I've had some help. Since 2014,

Rob Bell—renowned author, speaker, and former pastor—has been a steady, constant voice in my life. In the times when I've felt stuck, overwhelmed, or discouraged in my role as a pastor and speaker, Rob has been there to hear my struggles.

With his graceful tact, Rob has shepherded me through these years, helping me discover an inner wisdom, a Spirit guiding my path. When I first met Rob, I was mostly searching outside myself for answers and approval. I wasn't confident in what I possessed within. This was an exhausting way to live. By learning to look inside and trust this inner wisdom, I've come to discover a life that is more joyous and more true to the person I am.

No matter your beliefs, job, or passions, I believe this same life is available for you.

Told through eight years of email conversations between myself and Rob Bell (yes, Rob is well aware these emails are in print!), *Learning to Float* chronicles the countless questions I asked on my way to discovering a life of greater purpose and joy. While I understand my questions were specific to me, I've also seen how many of the questions and struggles we face are universal, revealing common longings we all carry. Longings for a life of authenticity and meaning. A life of joy that taps into the greatness we know we possess.

These conversations have helped me find just that. They've taught me how to float down the river of life by following my inner wisdom rather than drowning in weight and expectations that were never mine to carry. I hope they do the same for you.

Information Will Only Take You So Far

It all began at the start of 2014.

At the end of a two-day conference Rob had been hosting in California, I waited in line to ask if he ever did any one-on-one sermon coaching.

"Sure—send me an email, and we'll set it up," he replied, taking my phone to type in his email address. That didn't go so well.

While working in youth ministry a few years earlier, one of my students knew I was studying Hebrew in seminary. He decided to "help me out" by putting some weird setting on my iPhone that shifted the text pad from English to Hebrew with the push of a button. I could never figure out how to turn it off. While Rob was typing, he inadvertently transformed the whole keypad into Hebrew characters.

"I don't know what happened," he said, handing back the phone while telling me his email address.

As I walked away, red-faced, I wondered if Rob was already having second thoughts about giving his email address to some pastor who apparently took iPhone notes in Hebrew.

A week later, I was emailing him my most recent sermon, stomach tumbling with excitement and nervousness. Excitement about working with Rob to improve my craft. Nervousness over the fact I was new to this game. I had only been giving sermons regularly for a year, and my seminary training had included a single preaching class.

Sending Rob a sermon to critique left me feeling vulnerable. What would he say about my work? Would he think I had potential or tell me I should consider a new career?

From: **Dave Stradling**
To: Rob Bell
Date: January 18, 2014

Hey Rob!

This is Dave Stradling.

I was wondering if you'd be willing to listen to a few sermons and give some feedback. How much would that cost? I'm very interested in improving my speaking—I'd appreciate any help you could give.

Thanks!

Dave

From: **Rob Bell**
To: Dave Stradling
Date: January 21, 2014

*how about you send me one and i'll take a listen
and give you some feedback? (bro rate, which
means free!)*

Luckily, Rob saw potential. From the beginning, he could tell what I was speaking about mattered to me. I had "tremendous energy and passion" which was "crucial for this type of work." He then began walking me through the entire sermon, showing where I could have slowed down to bring the audience deeper into the ideas I was communicating. I was moving too fast, skimming the surface instead of pausing to explore the depths.

The main way I could grow, Rob said, was to move from information being the main part of a sermon to simply one of many tools in my box. To move from being an information giver to a guide, helping people see the world in a new way.

I was a young pastor in my early thirties when I first emailed Rob. Two years earlier, I'd started a church in my living room and was now hosting traditional Sunday morning services in a rented building.

Being young and inexperienced, I felt a strong need to prove myself. To others, yes. But also to myself. I was trying to prove I was worthy. Capable. That I had something to offer. I was trying to silence any self-doubt that I wasn't ready or good enough to be doing what I'd set out to do.

I did this through practices that came most naturally to me:

- reading

- learning

- studying

- accumulating knowledge.

By passing information onto others, I was trying to show how smart I was. To wow everyone with my brilliance.

I'll never forget one of those first Sunday mornings in my apartment. I was at my giant eight-foot whiteboard, in front of a small group, highlighting ten dualisms found in the Gospel of John. I was so excited to share this information. Surely I'd found some hidden insight that would blow everyone away.

Blank faces stared back at me.

From a young age, I was trained in an education system that largely rewarded you for how much you knew. This was the case in grade school, college, and seminary. I thrived in such a system and had the degrees and credentials to prove it. By working hard, I had achieved a level of success which led me to continue relying on that which had brought me to where I was: my intellect.

This approach initially shaped my understanding of a sermon. It was a means of transferring information. I never felt ready to preach until I'd read multiple books on the particular topic or Bible passage I was speaking on. Some weeks, I'd order books on Monday to read before I put together that week's sermon. I was expecting myself to become an expert purely through study.

Those early years were exhausting. I felt like Henry Bemis in the classic *Twilight Zone* episode "Time Enough at Last." It tells the brilliant story of a man who loves to read and sees everyone and everything as a distraction from this pursuit. There's never enough time for reading during the day . . . until . . . well, I won't ruin the ending. For me, there was never enough time to learn what I needed. I never felt fully prepared. I always felt like I should have studied more.

My early understanding of a sermon and the larger questions about spirituality, faith, and what it meant to be a pastor were reinforced by my ordination process. To become an officially licensed pastor, I had to pass a series of tests. One was a three-hour oral examination in front of a panel who judged whether I knew enough of the right answers to pass.

One of the first questions was, "Where is the love passage in the Bible?" I stumbled over my answer, saying it was either 1 Corinthians 13 or 14.

That didn't sit well with one of the panelists. He responded with, "If you want to have your driveway paved, what would happen if you gave them your neighbor's address? They would show up at the wrong house and you would have paid for your neighbor's driveway to be paved instead of yours."

I didn't know how to respond.

We moved on and that was how the topic of love was discussed in the interview.

As a fact.

An idea.

A fixed verse in the Bible.

There was nothing about how I or someone I knew had been transformed through an act of love. Nothing about how I had experienced God through love. Nothing about the fact that paying for your neighbor's driveway to be paved would be a great way to live out the love 1 Corinthians was talking about! It was about memory recall. Information.

During that interview, I saw how faith can be shaped by the larger systems we're a part of. It's not always intentional. It's a product of the academic, rational world we live in. A world that rewards you for possessing the correct information.

In this type of world, faith becomes about defending or proving ideas with facts instead of something to be experienced. It's lived in your head rather than through your life. This is where I was when I started out. I had a lot of information, and I saw my job as passing it along to others. I was equating life transformation with information. If I could just give everyone the right things to think and believe, their lives would be transformed.

A few months before I met Rob, I had planned to apply for a doctoral program. After completing a master's degree in biblical studies, I assumed the next step was to further my education. Gain more knowledge. Early one morning, I jumped on a train into New York City to spend a day visiting the school I was interested in. I sat in on a few classes, met with professors, and talked to current students. I loved the experience.

Yet, as I returned home on the train, I had an overwhelming sense that pursuing the degree was not the right step for me at the time. I couldn't explain why; I just knew it deep within. Later that week, I thanked everyone for their time and informed them I was going to hold off on the program.

Looking back, I see how I was being prepared for a new journey. A journey whose wisdom is not found at a desk piled with books. It can't be lived in your head through formulas, systems, and facts. This is a journey of experience. A journey whose wisdom is found as you slow down, listen, and open your heart.

Moving beyond Deconstruction

Wednesday, May 7, 2014

This next email made me cringe when I reread it. Immediately, I wanted to deny I was ever that person.

Was I really that hung up on those questions?

I can smile now when I think about where I was, but those struggles were real. They produced a lot of frustration within me. The type of church I wanted to create seemed so far out of reach.

From: **Dave Stradling**
To: Rob Bell
Date: May 7, 2014

Hey Rob,

Something I'm realizing is that I need to do more work defining exactly what we as a church are doing. I need more clarity for myself which will help those I'm leading as well.

From the beginning, I've wanted to create a church that is open and of a "generous orthodoxy." I want to create an environment where questions and rethinking the answers we've been given is OK, but I've already seen how we've lost people because of that. I felt called (and still do) to lead a church that breaks down some of the barriers that have prevented people from experiencing God but am struggling to see it happen. I want to see people's lives transformed as they become faithful followers of Jesus in the 21st century.

Any advice for how to move our group toward this type of faith? Is it that I simply need to do more work discerning exactly what I want to create, casting that vision, and being OK with losing people because it wasn't for them anyway? Ultimately I don't want to end up just maintaining a church of beliefs. I want to see transformation in lives and communities through the work we're doing.

Along with that tension, I'm having difficulty motivating people to live out their faith. With the feedback you gave me on my sermon, you suggested not giving people the "five things they could do to show love to their neighbor this week." Instead, you said to tell stories. I love that and am trying to tell more whenever I hear them, but I want to see and hear more. Any other ways to inspire/motivate people without telling them what to do? Do I need to give it time? How can I help the group become more attuned to hearing the Spirit in their lives?

Thanks for your time!

Dave

From: **Rob Bell**

To: Dave Stradling

Date: May 7, 2014

*ok, here's the deal: questions and rethinking are nice,
but people need help. right now.
with anger and love and revenge and stress and worry
and making sense of it all.
there are some things you believe, some things that drive
you, some things you know to be true.*

*for example, if a marriage is in trouble and then they get
help and work through it and the marriage starts to do better,
that's a good thing, right?*

*you can celebrate that, point to that, enjoy that. or to put
it another way, your job is to give people a vision of a new*

kind of jesus life. if you have to critique here and there the old vision for the purpose of clarity, that's probably fine, but only if it's in the service of the bigger thing you're doing. any energy you spend with them taking apart the old is time and energy you could be giving to building the new.

every time you encounter something that makes you think "this is why we do it," highlight it. have that person read their email to the church. have them tell that story they just told you. take a picture of it and show the folks and then tell them what you saw and how it inspires you. always get a name and a license plate number.

and then maybe you need to get more practical. maybe you need to give them assignments, for lack of a better word. maybe they need more direction, more guidance; maybe you need to end the sermon by giving them something to do and then the next week they tell what happened. you may be assuming they'll get it but they aren't there yet; they need more hand-holding, some training wheels. my "just tell stories" may not be enough to properly meet them where they're at. there may be things you naturally do that are totally foreign to them and so you have to break it down into the simplest steps and walk them through it . . .

does that help?

From: **Dave Stradling**

To: Rob Bell

Date: May 7, 2014

Yes, that makes sense and is helpful.

I need to be more aware of where the group is at and not try to make them be somewhere else.

I need to simplify with small steps.

So the questions and rethinking come as you paint a different picture than maybe what they've seen? It emerges from them as they are shown what this Jesus life looks like?

And my heart for those outside the church? For instance, I've had conversations with people where I've told them that I don't believe in a literal six-day creation and they'll sometimes wonder why more Christians can't be that open-minded. I want to be relevant and embracing of that group which has written off Christians and the Bible, but is that a concern that shouldn't even matter because I'm casting a vision for something that embraces both sides, and what we're doing helps people with the stuff that's bigger than that and relevant to the crap they're going through? Am I getting caught up on the wrong thing?

From: **Rob Bell**
  To: Dave Stradling
Date: May 7, 2014

excellent questions . . .
let's specifically address the six-day creation. it's important
for that person to know that you're open-minded, but the reason
is because you read the bible in the form that it comes in.
and when it's a poem, you read it like it's a poem.
and the reason you do that is because some truths
are bigger and deeper rather than literal.
they aren't about facts, they're about meaning.

and that's a truth everybody needs to hear.

the truth is, both the long-time christian and the person who isn't
a part of your church need the same thing. they're human, and
your job is to speak to the common humanity of both of them.

who doesn't want to worry less?
who doesn't want to be more loving?
who doesn't need help forgiving?
ask yourself what's true. period.
true, period. what's the thing that hits everybody?

think about both groups, talk to them both, keep sweating and
working and refining until you know that you're speaking
to both of them. you can do it. part of your ache is that
you have a vision for something that can be done,

you're on your way,
you're glimpsing something that not a lot of people
have the sight to see . . .

welcome to innovation.

Despite feeling stuck, I see how full of passion this email is. Passion is one thing I never lacked. I'll always remember one spring morning around the time I sent this email. I was sitting by myself on a park bench, wanting to quit the whole idea. But an internal spark, deep within, kept me holding on. I knew I had to keep going. I couldn't give up on what I felt inside.

Apparently, Rob could also sense my passion. He called it an "ache." This desire I had to create a church with space for everyone. To see real, lasting transformation in people's lives, whether they considered themselves Christian or not.

Back in the fall of 2010, I participated in a week-long assessment to see if starting a church was right for me. The feedback highlighted my "determination to do this." "You are going to do this whether we sponsor you or not," is what I was told. So, yeah, the passion's always been there.

While this is a good thing, I also stumbled upon the dark side of passion that exists when you don't find healthy ways to channel it.

Before starting a church, I organized a wine-and-cheese fundraiser to share my vision with some of my biggest supporters. I was hoping to gain financial support for this new church, Awaken. The next day, I asked a pastor what he thought of the evening. I carry his response with me to this day:

"Don't define yourself by what you're not."

He totally nailed it! I'd begun my talk by highlighting all the ways we weren't going to be like other churches. Instead of painting a beautiful, compelling picture of the church we were setting out to create, I'd spent my energy talking about the inadequacy of other churches and how we were going to do it better.

At the time, I was reading and learning so many new ideas that were reframing how I saw my faith. Starting a church was a response to what I was discovering. I wanted to create something that felt more aligned with my journey than some of the other expressions of faith I'd experienced.

While I truly believed I had the purest intentions, there was a big part of me that was merely reacting. I was in a deconstruction phase. Critiquing. Rethinking. Picking apart my theology to find all the pieces I no longer wanted to hold on to. I was fiercely passionate about this process, which left me with little energy for creating the type of church I envisioned or rebuilding my personal faith. I was more interested in proving how other ways were wrong.

Genesis 1 was the part of the Bible that started it all. I remember being shocked when my seminary professor, the great Dr. Widbin, described Genesis 1 as a poem.

Wait? There are other ways to read this part of the Bible than as a literal account of how the world was created? Yep. And plenty of people have noticed this fact.

This revelation handed me a whole new way to read the Bible. It was eye-opening, freeing, and upsetting all at the same time.

Why hadn't I been taught this before?

What else had I been missing?

From there, I set out to rediscover the Bible and what that meant for my faith.

When I started a church, I assumed everyone was on the same path of deconstruction as me. I soon learned how false that assumption was. I wanted to show others what I'd seen, but I was going about it all wrong. Instead of meeting people where they were in their lives, I was expecting them to be where I was.

Each person came with their own unique set of questions, fears, concerns, struggles, hopes, and desires. The rethinking worked well for some, but the majority of our group were just trying to make sense of where the divine presence was in their life.

Most people were there because they wanted a practical faith that helped them navigate the real-life struggles we all face on a weekly basis:

- tense relationships

- parenting concerns

- addictions

- feelings of shame

- loneliness

- anxiety

- apathy

- how to discover a life of meaning and joy

The last thing they were thinking about was how to classify the genre of Genesis 1. I was up in the clouds while people needed me on the ground with them.

Now, I was starting to see the need to move beyond deconstruction.

We recently had a flood in our basement from a clogged septic line. I woke up one morning to waste water covering the floor. Nasty stuff. The next day, a company came in to rip up the flooring, cut out some walls, and haul away everything damaged by the water. That is the current state of our basement—all torn up. There's no floor. No furniture. The wiring, studs, and pipes behind the walls are exposed. The space is unlivable.

Everything had to be torn out because of the damage. But we aren't going to leave the basement in that condition. We want to be able to use it again. Recently, a contractor came by to assess the basement. He took some measurements, we talked about how we wanted the space to look, and he'll soon get to work rebuilding.

Deconstruction is an important and necessary step. The problem was I had become stuck there. I was continuing to define myself by what I was against rather than what I was for. This kept me trapped in a cycle of tearing down, producing anger, cynicism, and arrogance within me. I was constantly on the lookout for ways to criticize others, showing how they were wrong and I was right. I had found the true path and saw it as my job to enlighten everyone else. This was not a great way to win friends and influence people. Nor was it leading to a place of inner joy. I was a lit fuse, constantly reacting to anyone or anything that reminded me of what I was leaving behind.

Those early years of trying to force my path onto others were frustrating. I was constantly wondering why people weren't getting it fast enough. Why weren't we growing? Why didn't more people want to deconstruct their faith? I had expected people to eagerly follow where we were going. That wasn't happening. Some would visit the church for a few weeks and never come back, while others were trying to figure out what in the world Dave was up to.

My expectations for others were removing the joy from my own life. My happiness was wrapped up in how people responded to me and the expectations I held for them. This was not a good formula. For me or the group.

During all of this, my passion never disappeared. It just needed a change in focus so I could fully invest my energy in shaping a faith that filled me with grace, peace, and love, while helping others discover the same.

The critiquing didn't go away completely either. There will always be ideas and actions that are wrong and harmful and damaging and destructive. They need to be called out. Wisdom comes from knowing when to critique and how to use it in a way that builds something better than what came before. The critique doesn't simply leave a void, rather it fills that void with something that is good, true, and healing for all people.

In May 2014 I was in the early stages of seeing all this. At the time I couldn't see any of it. I was in the middle of a forest, unable to see beyond the trees.

Sure, I was teaching about expectations, meeting everyone where they were, and "not defining yourself by what you're against." But these were merely concepts; ideas in my head that hadn't worked their way into my heart. I now see this was the moment when these ideas I had been living with began the long, slow descent into my heart.

Listening

Wednesday, July 16, 2014

Just two months after that last email, I was starting to see my role as a pastor differently. It was no longer all about my agenda or ego. It was becoming about the people I was pastoring. Meeting them in their space and helping them one step at a time.

From: **Dave Stradling**
  To: Rob Bell
Date: July 16, 2014

Hey Rob,

I've been giving some "assignments" to our group as a way to meet them where they are. Our convos have helped me realize I was thinking people were in different places than where they really are, so the assignments have been helpful.

Also, I'm learning that pastoring isn't so much about me accomplishing my agenda, but helping people deal with the realities already in front of them. I guess as my eyes are being opened to this, I've begun to see what people are truly going through.

Dave

From: **Rob Bell**
  To: Dave Stradling
Date: July 16, 2014

yes – you're doing great!

One big reason for this shift in my approach was that I started listening more. I had been so consumed with finding my value in how others responded to me, I had severed my ability to listen. Every conversation had been filtered through the points I wanted to get across and the information I wanted others to possess and believe.

I'd been steamrolling my way over others. Thinking more about how I was going to correct or respond instead of hearing someone's heart. It's never enjoyable to walk away from a conversation, wondering if the other person has heard a word you've said. Without realizing it, I'd been that other person.

Now, I was trying to understand people's very real needs. I was learning a new way of being. A whole different way of interacting with people.

I asked questions.

I tried to be slower to respond.

I allowed space for others to talk.

I slowly learned to sacrifice my need to "correct" others.

I gave space for others to feel comfortable bringing their entire self to the conversation.

All this birthed more compassion within me. It opened me up to the pain and hurt around me. For the first time, I was seeing what others were going through. The burdens they were carrying.

As I read this email now, I see how my earlier reactive self had prevented me from living this way. I was determined to prove other ways were wrong and have my voice heard the loudest. I thought I was following the true path of Jesus. In reality, I had found my own distorted path.

But this new path—I see it changing me. I can see my heart growing bigger.

The Exhaustion of Manufacturing Energy

Tuesday, September 16, 2014

For the next few months, I sailed along. It was exciting to finally have some clarity from the murkiness I'd been living with. I was inspired by all I was learning and this new path I was walking. It was only going to keep getting better.

Then this particular Sunday happened.

From: **Dave Stradling**
  To: Rob Bell
Date: September 16, 2014

Hey Rob!

This past Sunday, there was absolutely no energy in the room from the audience. It was bizarre. There was just this deadness coming from the crowd. This permeated the entire service. I had to manufacture all the energy for the sermon instead of being able to feed off the audience.

I tried to get them engaged, but nothing I tried worked. Is there anything I can do when that happens? Should I have stopped and acknowledged something? Is it just something that happens?

Even after, I was way more drained than usual. I could tell I had expended a lot of energy.

Thanks!

Dave

From: **Rob Bell**
To: Dave Stradling
Date: September 16, 2014

so here's the deal: this is normal. and it's not.

first the normal part. there will be sundays when the place is flat. dead. lifeless. when it feels like you're pushing a very large rock up a very large hill. all alone. in the rain. at night. you're going to do this for a while. you're playing the long game. this will happen from time to time when the people simply aren't crackling with energy. i saw a U2

show in chicago a few years ago that was so dead.
people were chatting between songs like we were
in a mall. U2 themselves apologized to their fans
a few years later for how bad that show was . . . so
in one sense it happens to everybody.

now, the not normal part. comedians talk about
killing it. you know why? because if you don't kill
it, it kills you. you have to be bigger than the room.
what happened sunday is the room defeated you.
whatever wasn't in the room was bigger and more
powerful than whatever WAS in you. get it? so
the real question isn't "why were they so dead?"
the better question is "what was wrong with what
i had to say?" because when it's a fire burning within
you, you let it rip with power and conviction and if
people don't respond, that is their problem not yours.

you had to manufacture. make a vow now you will
never ever manufacture ever again. preaching is
about tapping into the passion and fire that resides
in your belly that is bigger than you and channeling
it for others. the point is to get up there and open up
your heart AND DO YOUR PART. that is all you're
responsible for.

so what do you do in those moments? pause, take
a deep breath, and ask yourself WHY AM I DOING

THIS? make it really, really personal. remind yourself that you are practicing a craft, you are working a trade, you've got something to say and this is your work in the world. center yourself, smile, and then remember that these are defining moments. you got killed. next time you'll do the killing. when i'm somewhere now and the energy isn't good, i literally smile because i know this is one of those moments when i decide what kind of person i am becoming, what my fiber is, who i am, and the greatness i'm striving for . . . i've seen rooms turn around that were dead simply by me realizing in the moment that this is a test to see what i'm made of . . .

of course you were drained, you lost an epic spiritual battle. but you emailed me, which means you're not satisfied with defeat. which means there is greatness within you. so make a vow now that that will never happen again. the outcome isn't the point, the point is that your heart is more and more full of the divine indestructible love.

that help?

From: **Dave Stradling**
To: Rob Bell
Date: September 16, 2014

Yes, that helps! I really appreciate the encouragement. I didn't like the feeling of defeat nor did I like the feeling of "having to manufacture."

Thinking through it, I wasn't as ready as I should have been to get up there. My sermon didn't flow out of who I was becoming.

So yes, I vow to never let that happen again.

I'm seeing my inner life and who I'm becoming is just as important, if not more important, than what I'm saying.

If the audience embraces it, great. If not, I did my part because I can't control outcomes (I'm giving a gift from who I am and what I've learned and seen).

You mentioned an "epic spiritual battle." Is the battle internal or external or both?

From: **Rob Bell**
To: Dave Stradling
Date: September 16, 2014

great question.
two thoughts:
first, maybe there was something else going

*on in the room. that's not a crazy thought.
what's crazy is when people give that so much
weight and attention that they lose the plot.
so let's assume that sunday had lots of things
going on. the part you can control is your work.
your job is to stay true to the work you
have to do. the answer is yes, both.*

*second, what you're realizing is that your
inner life is the message. you were taught
a gospel that is announced, that exists
outside of you that you simply tell people
about. but the heart of the gospel is
incarnation, the message taking on flesh
and blood. you are the medium. you are
the message. and as your insides and
your outsides and your entire life becomes
more and more integrated and whole, your
message will become more and more powerful
because you're simply witnessing to the
life that is effortlessly flowing through you—
make sense?*

*so have hope. what happened this sunday
is shaping you into someone who isn't
phased by anything. next time you feel
the room like this, you'll pause, smile,
and feel a rush of spirit power because*

you'll realize this is one of those moments
that defines you. and you'll shine.

———————

From: **Dave Stradling**
  To: Rob Bell
Date: September 17, 2014

Yes, that makes perfect sense.

I've never thought about incarnation that way before.

Got a lot to think about.

The frustration was back. Here I was, giving it my all, summoning all the energy and enthusiasm I could muster, but my words seemed to fall on deaf ears. There was no life in the room. Naturally, I defaulted to placing the blame on others.

Why weren't they getting it?

Why wasn't everyone jumping out of their seats in excitement about the sermon I was giving?

I was pouring out everything I had and people were scrolling through their Instagram feed.

Normalizing this experience while calling me out at the same time was so helpful. Rob had exposed the flaws in my thinking. I was asking the wrong questions. Blaming others when I should have been looking into myself.

"Manufacture energy" is the phrase I used in my original email. That is so telling. It communicates work. Hard work. Draining work because of the amount of energy being expended. I was trying to create something that wasn't there before. If I was "manufacturing energy," I was looking outside myself for what I needed rather than accessing the life happening within.

As Rob helped me see this, I began noticing how I felt when giving a sermon. If I felt off, it was usually because I wasn't preaching from my personal experience. I was preaching someone else's truth. Speaking on ideas I hadn't experimented with in my own life. Ideas I hadn't personally discovered to be true.

"Disconnected" is the word that best describes this feeling. There was a disconnect between what I was communicating and what I experientially knew to be true. My head and heart weren't connected.

Around this time, I ran across an article highlighting how one of my all-time favorite authors, James A. Michener, prepared to write his novel *Chesapeake*. Michener, known for his massive historical fiction works, always spent a good amount of time in the physical location he was planning to write about. He didn't want to solely read about a country's history and culture; he wanted to experience it for himself.

The sights.

Sounds.

Smells.

Food.

Conversations with locals.

For *Chesapeake*, he bought a house on a creek near the entrance to the Chesapeake Bay and lived there for three years as he researched and wrote the novel. This, according to Michener, is what it took to write a story true to the land he was writing about. The story originated from his experiences instead of facts in a book. I'm sure this is why I enjoy his novels so much. The details and characters are full of life because he has taken the time to live with them long before he put his typewriter to use.

When I started pastoring, I was excited about everything I was learning. I came home from conferences with pages of notes. All my books were highlighted with pages folded over and insights written on the back flap. I'd immediately want to share with everyone the best of what I'd stumbled upon, whether in conversations or my sermons.

But then the follow-up questions came. Or, I'd be in the middle of a conversation and realize I had absolutely no idea what I was talking about. I hadn't taken the time to think through what I was sharing. Hadn't considered the implications. Even worse, I'd sometimes be in the middle of a sermon when I would start thinking, *This really isn't as interesting as I originally thought.* There'd be a sinking feeling in my gut as I fumbled my way to the finish line. In my excitement, I wasn't taking the time to explore the depths of what I was learning. I wasn't living long enough with the ideas I was preaching.

A big reason for this was my life was filled with studying. Each week, I felt an all-consuming anxiety to have something new and groundbreaking to say. It was an ever-present storm cloud hovering over me. The only way I knew to ease the anxiety was to gather more information and find out what others had said. I didn't believe in myself. I had no trust in the person I was or the Spirit within me that I spoke about each week, so I defaulted to looking outside myself for what to say.

I went directly from books to sermons. There was no space in my life to put into practice what I was learning or to let these ideas marinate within. I was endlessly cramming myself full of information for a looming sermon.

With all this studying, those early preaching days often saw me finishing my sermons on Saturday nights. It was exhausting. I hated it. Sitting there alone in whatever room of the house I was using as an office while my wife, Steph, was out with friends or on the couch watching a movie. Week after week it continued, with no other staff to help with the preaching responsibilities.

After writing my sermon, I'd wake up the next day, give the sermon, and then start the process all over again Monday morning as I sat staring at a blank page. It's a wonder I had any energy left by Sunday morning.

Sending this email to Rob was a recognition that how I'd been approaching my sermons wasn't working. Instead of killing it, I was getting killed most weeks. Yet, despite how I was feeling, a resilience and dissatisfaction with defeat burned inside me. Rob could sense this and pointed it out. I wasn't going to give up now.

But, he wasn't letting me off the hook. Just from the words I used in my email, he knew what was happening. Twice he told me to take a vow. I took that seriously. If he was going to be that direct, I knew I had to pay attention. There was a better, more life-giving way to live. Not a life outside myself that I had to manufacture and work for. Or a life I could understand from the experiences of others. Rather, this was a life that flows from within.

A life that flows out of my own experiences with the Spirit.

First, You're a Student

Six months went by, during which time I began to make a shift in my sermons. I began to share more. I was having more fun as I opened my life and began to trust what was inside me. However, this was raising another layer of questions.

Once, I'd been in church when the pastor turned the sermon into his own personal counseling session. There was a stunned, awkward silence as we all sat listening uncomfortably while he publicly processed his life.

I knew this wasn't what I wanted, but where was the line between what to share and what to leave out? How would I know how deep into my story to go?

From: **Dave Stradling**
  To: Rob Bell
Date: March 5, 2015

Hi Rob,

Things are going well and I'm feeling more confident in my speaking. We've seen growth, but more importantly, people are beginning to experience healing and a new outlook on both faith and life. I'm getting over my need to have everyone "rethink" faith and have been focusing more on leading people to wholeness through my teaching.

People have responded well and we have great stories of families being more present with each other. One father took extra months off from his job to be with his newborn baby and wife who was diagnosed with cancer at the same time that their baby was born. He said he never would have been able to do that a year ago but has embraced a lot of what we are talking about and has a whole new outlook on his life and what is truly important.

I do have a question I'm wrestling with right now. How do I know how much of my story to share? I'm working on an upcoming sermon for Lent where I'm talking about embracing doubts and questions as a way to resurrection. That's been a big part of my faith shift as I've had experiences in which everything didn't work out the way I was told it was supposed to. So I want to use part of my story in the sermon, but I'm afraid sharing too much might do more harm than good at this point.

Do you have any suggestions/guidelines as I work on this? I know it's different for every group, but how can I determine the right balance between knowing what's the right amount to share, creating some tension, but not harming anyone's faith?

Thanks!

Dave

———————

From: **Rob Bell**
To: Dave Stradling
Date: March 6, 2015

good question! and great update!

couple of thoughts
first, with any topic, ask yourself:
what have i learned about this?

you are a teacher, but first you are a student.
so what have you learned and how can you bless us
with that gift?
just asking questions or sharing your pain and
wondering about stuff—anybody
can do that. what we need is your wisdom.

second, if it feels like too much, then it is.

third, once you share it, you can't unshare it.
so whatever you're thinking about sharing,
run it by someone. you will know immediately by the look on
their face whether that belongs in a sermon, trust me.

fourth, the point is not thinking but living—so everything
comes down to whether or not it taps you into the divine
life that is the beating heart of the universe.

boom!

From: **Dave Stradling**
  To: Rob Bell
 Date: March 7, 2015

OK, thanks—that helps a lot!

Never thought of being a student before being a teacher.
I guess I knew it intuitively but it helps to have that as an
intentional lens through which to view my teaching.

I've been leaning less on commentaries and books
recently and more on my experiences and the wisdom I
already possess, so that is a great affirmation for me.

From: **Rob Bell**
 To: Dave Stradling
Date: March 8, 2015

yes yes yes—remember that when jesus talked about knowing the truth, he said it was if you hold to his teaching. in other words, if you live a certain way, then you will have had experiences and you'll know certain things are true because you've lived them.

the greek word he uses for "know" means firsthand experience. only preach what you've experienced and your sermons will be so much more fun to preach!

––––––

From: **Dave Stradling**
 To: Rob Bell
Date: March 9, 2015

That's a complete paradigm shift. But one that makes perfect sense and that I'm discovering to be true.

Totally just opened up a whole new way of thinking for me.

I had a blast with yesterday's sermon because it was truly birthed from within me rather than working from the outside in.

Rob's practical advice helped tremendously. Not only did he provide insight into the questions I was wrestling with, but he also opened up a new way for me to understand my role as a teacher. "You are a teacher, but first you are a student . . . we need your wisdom."

I have a good friend who sometimes gives sermons in my absence. The first time he spoke, he asked, "What do you want me to speak on?"

I responded, "Just tell your story, bro."

If it wasn't all about information, I thought, it must be about telling others what I've been through. I was missing the wisdom piece.

Being real and honest about my life was necessary, but it couldn't end there. It couldn't just be about "telling my story." Every personal detail. Each part of my journey I shared had to serve a larger purpose. It had to be mined for what I'd discovered so I could offer wisdom and practical steps to help others walk through similar experiences.

To do this, I had to become a student of my life.

I started approaching every sermon through this new lens. I asked questions like:

- What stories do I have about my experiences with this idea?

- What have I learned through that personal experience?

- What have I found to be true about the topic I'm speaking on?

- What practical steps have helped me experience the truths I'm communicating?

The gift of preaching, I was discovering, is helping others see what I've seen. This requires a deep level of awareness of the lessons learned along the way. And it requires space in my life for that awareness to arise.

Everything I was learning was not only changing my speaking but also the entire foundation of my life. It all led to some pretty significant shifts in my understanding of faith. For the longest time, I had believed the Christian faith to be about possessing the right doctrine. Just look at my previous emails and my educational background. I was so focused on ideas and intellectual truths that existed in my head.

Now, I was discovering the Christian faith to be about walking a particular path. The way to truth wasn't through intellectual assent, believing a whole set of ideas that can be argued and debated. Instead, truth is found through experience.

Jesus's words in the Gospel of John began to come alive in an entirely new way. "If you hold to my teaching, you are really my disciples. Then you will know[1] the truth, and the truth will set you free." (John 8:31–32)

Yes, the invitation of Jesus is one of trust. But not trusting in ideas. Trusting in his way of living. Jesus's teachings were practical. He embodied a particular way of living and invited others to do the same. By putting into practice his teachings, Jesus was promising you would come to know the truth in your own life. And it would lead to a life of freedom. One marked by grace and peace and love. A life lived in harmony with the Spirit.

---

1   In the original Greek language, this is the word *ginosko* Rob referred to in his email, meaning to know something through firsthand experience.

The life transformation I desired to see in others and myself was not going to come by acquiring more information. Or by getting others to subscribe to a certain set of beliefs. Instead, true transformation, according to Jesus, comes by living in particular ways. Your life then naturally begins to embody truth.

As a pastor, my role was to invite others into trusting the way of Jesus. The only way I could authentically do this was by having my own personal experiences with the teachings of Jesus and report back to others what I was learning. Gifting them with the tools and truths I was discovering through firsthand experience. All so others could have their own personal experiences and discover for themselves the truth Jesus spoke about.

At the time, we were creating a new website for our church. An important part of every church website is the "beliefs" section. However, as I was learning all this, the idea of a beliefs section for our website felt static. It was flat, one dimensional. I was discovering that you could believe a whole bunch of statements but still not know the truth. I've also seen how divisive beliefs can be. They act as sentries, allowing some people in while keeping others out. I didn't want that. From the beginning, I wanted to create a church with room for everyone, regardless of where they found themselves on the belief spectrum.

After thinking about it for a while, I decided to use two of the earliest Christian creeds as the foundation of our church: the Apostles' Creed and the Nicene Creed. I then added this disclaimer, which I still love all these years later:

> But while we affirm these statements of faith, we recognize that reading a statement of faith isn't the best way to discover what a group believes.

Instead, it is best to join that group in action. We therefore invite you to join us on this journey to live out the words of Jesus in the twenty-first-century culture in which we find ourselves.

Imposter Syndrome

Monday, February 15, 2016

When I started a church, I was always surprised when a new person walked through the door and even more shocked to see them return the next week. I wanted the church to grow, but I didn't believe it would happen. Maybe this was because we were so small for those first few years. Whenever a visitor came back, I'd immediately wonder why they would choose to become involved in what I'd created. Why would anyone be interested in what *I* had to say about spirituality?

I had a taste of this even earlier, during the first sermon I ever gave in my early twenties. I was on stage, delivering my sermon while looking out at the group of adults gathered to hear what I had to say. A few minutes in, I noticed one woman was scribbling away in a notebook. I soon realized she wasn't just doodling. She was taking notes. Notes? Really? She thought I had something to say that was worth writing down so she could refer to it later? It was a surreal experience. Why would anyone want to take notes on what I was saying?

Years later, I discovered what I was experiencing in those early years was "imposter syndrome." It's when you doubt yourself. You worry that somehow you will be exposed as a fraud. In my case, I didn't believe I had anything of value to say. There were plenty of others wiser than me. I was just Dave Stradling from Somers, NY. What did I know? I now realize this is why I spent so much time relying on the wisdom of others. On my own, I wasn't good enough.

From: **Dave Stradling**

To: Rob Bell

Date: February 15, 2016

Hey Rob,

I usually listen to my sermon each week as a way to critique myself. One habit I've noticed for a while is that I tend to end a lot of my sentences with an upward inflection which makes it feel like I'm unsure about what I'm saying. Could you recommend any ways that I can work on the delivery of my sermons? Is it just about continued repetition, practicing more before I deliver it, or are there any specific practices that I can do in order to improve my delivery? I'm loving the work of putting content together and then delivering it. I now want to move to the next level in the area of delivery.

Should I practice the whole thing in front of someone, record it, and watch/listen to myself?

Thanks!

Dave

From: **Rob Bell**
  To: Dave Stradling
Date: February 15, 2016

you're probably ending your sentences
like that because you aren't confident.
one question to ask:
is your sermon you witnessing to what
you have actually experienced?
Only preach what you've lived.
Tell them what you felt and saw.
Tell them what you have learned.
That help?

From: **Dave Stradling**
  To: Rob Bell
Date: February 16, 2016

Yeah, this was definitely material that I've experienced,
but for some reason I feel as if I still kept myself at arm's
length from the content and it felt rigid, even a personal
story that I told. I've been given this feedback before and
see it being a trend.

I think I'm still wrestling through who I am and why anyone should listen to what I have to say. Even though the church is growing and we are attracting older adults and high-level leaders, I still struggle with the confidence piece. Anything I can do to break through this? Silence/meditation? Having someone yell in my ear "you can do this" before I preach?

I guess this is more subconscious than a "practice more" issue.

———————————

From: **Rob Bell**
   To: Dave Stradling
 Date: February 16, 2016

exactly. it's a confidence thing. here's the thing:
you're never going to figure it out.
let me say that again.
you're never going to figure it out.
why are you in charge?
why do you get paid to say spiritual things?
why do they listen?
why do you get to live such a fantastic life?

do you see your problem? you're actually trying to make sense of it. you're stuck in your head. you're insecure about your voice. you're trying to figure it out.

now here's the truth: life doesn't exist as an intellectual category. it's not an abstract thought to be made sense of. it's your life. and you get to preach. which means the only thing left to do is enjoy it.

do you get that?
you get to enjoy this.
there will always be someone smarter and wiser and more experienced and better educated. that will never go away.

but you can throw yourself into your life.
you don't need someone to say "you can do this."
you need someone to say
"you get to do this."

so relax. who cares? we're all going to die. some people are going to leave your church. some are going to criticize you. some are going to hear you once and never come back. some are going to listen to every sermon you've ever done and then you're going to realize that they haven't heard anything!

see what i mean?

all that's left to do is enjoy it.

why should anyone listen to you?

*because you're having a blast. because you've found
something you're thrilled to share. because you love your life.
because you're enjoying yourself and that's what
everyone wants.*

get out of your head.

*but most of all, enjoy it. relax. loosen up. it's all a crapshoot.
you'll never be able to answer the questions of why, but you
can give it all you got.*

From: **Dave Stradling**
  To: Rob Bell
Date: February 16, 2016

Thanks, Rob!

That's really helpful, I appreciate the advice and encouragement.

I still try to rationalize too much. I'll focus less on the why
and more on the pure joy of getting to do what I do and
throwing myself into that!

It really is much more freeing to look at it that way than as
an intellectual category I need to figure out and control,
which is a waste of time, energy, and joy.

For years, I worked with a life coach. During one session, I asked his opinion about an upcoming decision I had to make for the church. After telling him what I was thinking, he told me to go for it! He then followed up by inviting me to trust my intuition more. "I have never once thought your intuition was off," he told me.

Our conversation ended, but I kept replaying his words in my head. I knew the decision I had to make. The wisdom was within me, but I needed the approval, the permission of someone else before I acted on it. I was looking outside myself for answers I already possessed.

This haunting inner struggle was showing up in how I presented myself to others. Especially in my sermons. It was as if there was a voice in the back of my head relentlessly asking, "What if you're wrong?" or "What if you say something that others disagree with?"

A big reason for this insecurity was the deconstruction journey I was on. I wasn't confident in the personal path I was walking. I was leaving behind pieces of my faith tradition, but I wasn't fully confident that the faith I was reconstructing was "right." I would often wonder whether I even knew anything about the faith in which I was supposed to be leading others. I was the pastor. The one who was supposed to offer certainty. And here I was trying to figure out my own faith.

One Sunday morning, as I was speaking, two visitors stood up in the middle of my sermon, walked out the door, and never came back. This bothered me for weeks after. In my head, I created a story about them not liking what I was saying. Maybe it was true, but maybe it wasn't. I never had the chance to find out.

At the time, our services took place in hotel conference rooms. The visitors who walked out might have been hotel guests who had stumbled upon our service, decided to check it out for a few minutes before leaving for a flight, and stayed longer than expected because they were enjoying it so much.[2]

Two completely different stories. I chose to believe the one that spoke of my inadequacy.

For the most part, this internal struggle existed below the surface of my awareness. I was still so focused on external elements, believing I'd improve my speaking by practicing more or finding the right formula. But now I see how much of a role my inner life plays in my speaking. I'm being led deeper within and uncovering the stories that have been shaping me.

Mixed in with my constant need for approval and self-doubt came a whole host of internal questions about why I was getting paid to do something I loved. I would frequently hear about people disliking their jobs or having a daily train commute for hours into New York City for a job they weren't in love with.

Hearing these stories made me feel guilty. I loved the work I was doing, even if it left me tired and disappointed at times. I knew this was what I wanted to be doing with my life. But why was *I* so lucky? Why did I deserve to do something I enjoyed that paid the bills while others didn't have that same opportunity?

The exhaustion!

Mentally and physically.

I see now the weight I was carrying around with me. I always wondered why those beginning years left me so exhausted. Clearly, it was my own inner battle tiring me out. I believed it

---

2   Huge thanks to Ron Martoia for helping me see the story in this light!

was all about proving my worth and trying harder, doing more so I was deserving of the position I was in. I was so afraid of losing everything that I was forgetting to live.

This led to preaching becoming more of a chore than a joy. I was trapped in a system of my own making.

Overthinking.

Overanalyzing.

Second-guessing myself.

Trying to find answers to questions that were unanswerable.

For so long, I'd been in my head trying to figure it all out. I was searching for answers that no one could provide. But life isn't meant to be figured out. There's far too much messiness to ever have it tied up in a nice neat package. There's a mystery. An irrationality. An unpredictability to it all. Sometimes it lands on black, sometimes red. And no one will ever know why.

I knew this. I had experienced plenty of moments when questions were left unanswered. Questions I knew would never find an answer. Yet, here I was, seeking the elusive "why." All it did was drain my energy and take me further away from life.

Life, Rob helped me see, is something to be experienced. This can't happen in your head. It happens as you enter into the fullness of each moment for the beauty (and tragedy) it can bring. That is where the joy is found.

Yes, it could all be taken from me at any moment—the church, preaching, life itself—but that's what makes it all so beautiful. It's here one moment, gone the next.

I'm not sure where I adopted this fear-based way of living. I look back at pictures when I was younger and see a different person than who I am now. I was free. Filled with joy. Experiencing my life. Not consumed with figuring it all out.

When I broke my leg playing soccer in high school, I switched to playing tennis because it was non-contact and about the only sport the doctor would let me play. In high school, tennis wasn't considered the cool kids' sport, but I embraced it. I became co-captain and soon our team was wearing red Hawaiian shirts for our matches that I had picked out. We were known as "The Flying Hawaiians."

I started a punk band called 30 Foot Salmon. No matter how much I tried to delude myself, deep down I knew it wouldn't last long, so I soaked up every minute—every practice, every show, every time I'd sit down with my thesaurus and marble notebook to write song lyrics. I gave it my all. Jumping too high in practice one night and splitting my head open on a metal support beam, four staples in my scalp—no problem. I was back the next week, ready to go stronger than ever.

Somewhere, I had lost my way. And I was going to keep searching until I found the truest version of myself.

The Power of Presence

By this time, I'd settled into a system for writing sermons. Every week I'd sit at my desk typing out a six-page manuscript. I had learned this was the right number of pages for a thirty-minute sermon. From there, I worked hard to memorize my manuscript right down to the exact wording of specific sentences. It was a tiring, repetitive process. One that took place mostly in my office in front of a computer screen.

When Sunday morning rolled around, I'd stand in front of my congregation with an outline of my manuscript, trying to look at it as little as possible. I wanted to show others I knew what I was talking about and didn't need notes as a crutch. Mastery of the material, I thought, meant I had committed it to memory. I spent the entire sermon in my head as I willed myself to remember every last detail like an end-of-semester final exam. And, just like those exams, this process was every bit as anxiety producing. I had to perform well because everyone was watching! I was like a nervous tightrope walker terrified of falling.

Giving sermons had become, for me, the equivalent of test-taking. Before a test, you cram as much information as possible into your head so you'll have all the right answers. Usually, this cramming happens the night before a big test, or the morning of it. While the cramming may help for short-term memory recall, very rarely does that information stay in your head for weeks or months after.

It's memorized,

regurgitated,

then forgotten.

This is what I had turned my sermons into. This approach worked in college. Why wouldn't it work for the weekly test I had to take each Sunday morning?

As time went on, I became aware that something was off in my speaking. I was noticing a feeling of disconnect. I'd sit down after speaking and feel as though I hadn't given the sermon. Like the times you pull into your driveway having forgotten the entire ride home from work. You know it happened but can't recall the experience.

My energy and attention were so focused, so consumed, on remembering every little detail, I wasn't able to be fully present during the sermon.

Physically I was there. Spiritually and mentally, I was somewhere else.

From: **Dave Stradling**
  To: Rob Bell
Date: October 17, 2016

Hey Rob!

Hope you're doing well! I'm absolutely loving the speaking aspect of pastoring. I feel I'm starting to find my groove and have truly found the thing that I want to give my life to.

Something I've noticed with my speaking recently is that I still rely too much on having a very detailed structure for my sermon. I end up manuscripting most of it out and then giving the sermon without any notes. I'm able to memorize the basic outline and have no problem with recollection, but I feel I'm not as free because my brain is confined by too many details I'm trying to remember.

I've heard you talk multiple times on having an outline for a sermon but not writing all the details down. Any guidance you can give on how to get to that point? I feel the writing of all the details, even certain sentences, is like a security blanket that I'm ready to shed in order to move to the next level of my speaking.

Thank you!

Dave

From: **Rob Bell**
To: Dave Stradling
Date: October 18, 2016

*you're probably packing too much into the sermon
and moving too fast.
this is often what happens when you start having things
to say!
i've seen this before: you suddenly realize that there is all
this great truth and you get to say it.
so think about this:
the simplicity after complexity.
you're stuck in the complexity.
what is the simplicity on the other side?
are there three movements?
four parts?
break it down structurally into its biggest chunks,
then,
what are the parts within those big parts?
how many are there?
at the end, the outline that i have is actually really simple.
i've done a three-hour talk and on the piece of paper were
four words.
so what you're learning to do is trust that the details
will come in the moment.
so part of the new thing for you is to put the outline away
an hour before the sermon and sit in silence,
and still your mind and heart,*

and be in the sermon.
sit in it.
feel it instead of thinking it.
spend more time getting quiet and still
because when you're centered and grounded
all those details will come to you in the moment,
but only if they add,
not if they're clutter.

it sounds like your sermons are too cluttered right now.
the answer isn't so much in outlining
as it is in centering and stilling
so that you'll learn to trust yourself.
that whatever detail you need in that moment
will be available to you.
slow down
slow down
slow down

boom
that help?

From: **Dave Stradling**
  To: Rob Bell
Date: October 19, 2016

Yes, this helps! I have a hard time trusting that the details will come in the moment, which is why I try to write it all down and cram it all in my head, causing me to be more focused on recalling how I wrote it rather than feeling my way through the sermon. I'm seeing more and more how the way in which you set up your life and live directly impacts your speaking and the presence you bring to it.

I'm guessing my sermons sometimes feel long or cluttered because I'm moving too fast over things rather than giving more depth. When it feels like that, should I cut and try to narrow my focus more? Tell another story, give more detail on a particular idea, etc.?

From: **Rob Bell**
  To: Dave Stradling
Date: October 20, 2016

yes, exactly, you're probably going too fast.
remember that people have a thousand burdens
and thoughts and anxieties.

here's a new thing for you to try: think about the
sermon like architecture. like you're building a space
out of words. a space where doubt and fear and anger

*and love and joy and compassion and hope can all
sit side by side. because that's what your people are
bringing to the space on sundays. so think about what
kind of space your sermon is going to create.*

*whatever you do, don't rush them through the space.
you create and you point out some art on the walls and
you also leave room for them to see and hear and experience
things you hadn't even noticed yet.*

*so one of your problems is you are getting fired up by the
sermon and writing down every thought this great new idea
spurred in you—those are the details—but you have to give
people a chance to have the same inspiring experience
you did!*

*so think back to how you first encountered whatever it is
that you're excited to preach about. show them what you
have seen and tell them some ways it has moved you and
give them some suggestions for where it may take them
and then let the space breath.*

*trust. that's the thing for you.
trust that if you are deep in the soul of this thing and you
are true to it, they'll have profound glimpses as well.*

*so it's less, which is more.
make sense?*

From: **Dave Stradling**
  To: Rob Bell
Date: October 20, 2016

Yes, this makes sense. This gives me a bunch to work on.

I think I'm beginning to discover my voice, and I am excited I get to share what I've seen!

Now it's learning how to pull back a bit so others can have that same experience rather than be fire-hosed.

The first pastor I worked for would often say that, when giving a sermon, "you must first connect with yourself." It took me years to grasp the wisdom in this truth. In those early years, I wasn't connecting with myself. My sermons were still information-based. Even though I was presenting material true to me and my experiences, I was turning it into ideas to be memorized and passed along while neglecting the soul of what I was communicating.

I was skimming the surface, moving too fast, instead of inviting others into the depths of the truths I was speaking on.

This was a product of how I was living.

My life was

hurried,

cluttered,

scattered,

shallow.

Of course this would make for

hurried,

cluttered,

scattered,

shallow sermons.

It's who I was inside.

I was always feeling rushed.

Always feeling pressured.

Always on the go, moving from one thing to the next with little time or space to connect with myself.

I had made *doing* a priority over *being*.

One particular Saturday, Steph and I were driving from a lunch with members of the church to a birthday party for a family member. Rushing to the party because we were late, we looked at each other and said, "We can't do this anymore." We no longer wanted to live feeling hurried all the time. Saying yes to everything and cramming in as much as we could. We knew there had to be a better, less anxious way to live. I just couldn't find a way to access that life.

When I think about presence, I think about the effect someone has on your being. There are some people I want to be around because they inspire me. When I'm with them, I feel energized. Ready to accomplish anything. Others exude a sense of calmness that's contagious. Then there are others who leave me feeling drained. Like I've just given my all in a marathon. Others project such a high level of anxiety, I walk away feeling like a tangled string of Christmas lights.

Presence is the unspoken energy we all give off. It's a powerful communicator of who we are inside that speaks louder than our words.

It's how we intuitively feel when someone isn't being truthful.

Or why we can walk into a room and know two people have just had a fight, even though they assure you everything is great. Our presence can permeate a room.

It's how you show up in the world. And how you show up in the world is an expression of who you are inside.

It can reveal depth or shallowness.

Calmness or anxiety.

If I wanted to be an inspiring, calm presence simply by being in the room, even before I opened my mouth, I had to bring that presence with me. I was seeing more and more how integrated all of life is. My sermons weren't just about the thirty minutes on a Sunday morning. It wasn't about finding the perfect outline. It was about creating a life in which I had space to breathe.

So, I started with one small step.

Instead of poring over my manuscript Sunday mornings up until the moment I gave my sermon (and I literally mean the moment), I began to go through it once in the morning before putting it away for good. Then, I would go for a walk around the neighborhood and feel my way through every part of the sermon as a way to connect with myself. I was trying to slow down. To be still and silent. To lessen the anxiety that cramming produces, so I would bring a less hurried and more calm presence with me.

Of course, this was a small step, and there were plenty of other steps to take, but this is where I started. I did this every Sunday morning—no matter the weather—except for the morning a black bear sauntered across our neighbor's front lawn on my way out the door. I stayed inside that day.

And you know what immediately happened?

Nothing much.

There was no miraculous moment when everything changed. For a while, I actually felt more vulnerable. *Wait, I can't look at my notes while everyone is greeting each other right before I start?! I can't cram up until the last minute?*

The discomfort, I soon realized, came because I was learning to trust in something other than myself, my hard work, and how well I could memorize ideas. I was learning to trust the Spirit.

And that is another lesson best learned by having it all come crashing down around you.

Euchaɾiʂt Living

During my high school and college years, I worked at a car garage. One piece of wisdom I learned from my time there was the importance of refilling your gas tank before the low-fuel light comes on. Best practice is to pull into the station when you hit a quarter tank. This protects the fuel pump from working too hard and causing problems down the road.

I was well aware that I was long overdue for a fill-up. That was why I sent this next email. My gas light had been on for miles and the gas gauge was hitting the empty line. I just didn't do anything about it. I kept going, forcing that fuel pump to work harder as I squeezed out every last drop of fuel in the tank.

People had been leaving the church, and their departure was taking its toll on me. The initial spark that had compelled me into this work was missing. I knew it. I could feel the heaviness upon me.

The problem was, I wasn't allowing myself to be honest with how I was feeling. Instead of acknowledging the pain of loss, all I felt was guilt for not being as passionate as I once was.

From: **Dave Stradling**

To: Rob Bell

Date: April 24, 2017

Hey Rob!

I'm struggling to get my groove back. These past few weeks of speaking have been a drain and a battle.

Over the past four months, there's been a bunch of people from the church who have left or are in the process of leaving and it's been draining watching people leave after having invested so much in them.

I feel this soul tiredness that pervades my work right now. How do I get that spark back? There are a bunch of new ideas that I'm excited about pursuing and I love the material I'm preaching on, but I just don't feel like I have the energy to give my best to these projects. I know I'm not at the top of my game and I can't shake this tiredness and general weariness. Does that excitement/weariness make sense?

I've even thought about pursuing something different because I want to feel alive again. I love speaking and helping open people's eyes and I want to be in it for the long run, just not feeling this way.

Thanks,

Dave

From: **Rob Bell**
  To: Dave Stradling
Date: April 24, 2017

it does make sense.
you're grieving.
these people were friends. you gave them time,
energy, love, etc
and now they're gone
which, no matter what anyone says,
is a form of death.
you're grieving.
and grieving is exhausting.
it's a season. and it will pass, and it will pass
sooner the more honest you are about it.
so you haven't been seeing it as grief and you've
been continuing to live your life like you always do
and the first thing to go is desire. passion. spark.
so put the brakes on.
eat good food. sleep in. long runs or walks. watch
some movies. do the bare minimum. do what sounds
pleasurable. fill your soul.
part of what is so draining is that you keep asking
"why am i so tired?
that question is tiring!
you're tired because you're going through a death

and that needs to be grieved.
so give it the space it needs.

one more note: you give the gift because that's where
the life is. you're wondering why you gave these people
all that time and energy if they were going to leave you.
but that's the transaction view of the world: we do things
to get things back.
but you're in eucharist.[3] you give the gift because that's
where the life is. no guarantees on who will get it and
stay or walk away.
so take care of yourself. relax. do what fills the tank.
be in this season and feel whatever you need to.
that help?

From: **Dave Stradling**
  To: Rob Bell
Date: April 25, 2017

Yes, that helps. I feel like I intuitively knew that, yet while
I've been doing less because that's all I can do, I've been
feeling guilty about it which is probably making me even

---

3   Eucharist is a Christian ritual regularly practiced to remember the
    death of Jesus on the cross. Eucharist comes from two Greek words,
    eu and *charis*, meaning "good gift." Eucharist remembers the good
    gift of Jesus' life freely given in love for the healing of our world.

more tired. Thanks for the permission to be fully in this season and feel what I'm going through.

I need to listen more to what I'm feeling instead of barreling through and continuing on like everything's normal. I've definitely noticed myself wanting to go more into transactional living rather than Eucharist living during these few months—guess that feeling is normal with grieving, and means I need to slow down and refill.

Now that I've been doing this a while, I'm really seeing how integrated the whole speaking process is. The information is the easy part—it's the inner preparation that is the real challenge.

Thank you!

Dave

From: **Rob Bell**
  To: Dave Stradling
Date: April 25, 2017

well said.
and never forget: this is what comes with
this work.
so go with it.
do what you need.
and never defend or apologize.
this is serious work.

and you're starting to get serious.
and that means you're getting serious
about time away and time off and rest
and spending the whole day walking
in the woods.
that's part of taking this seriously—
taking care of yourself and doing whatever
you need to do to stay healthy and sane.

It's hard to not take it personally when someone walks away from something you've created. This church that I created felt like a part of me. It was a tangible expression of who I was and I was giving it everything I had. I was feeling abandoned after having given a part of myself.

Getting to a place of "Eucharist" living, where I would give with no expectations, sounded so free, but I wasn't there yet. I was still stuck in expectations: expectations about how I wanted others to respond to me and how to personally respond to what I was going through.

Somewhere, I had picked up the belief that I was to keep pushing my way through whatever obstacle I faced. Maybe it was my pastor training. I was the spiritual leader, the one with an unwavering faith that could carry me through anything. Maybe it stemmed from the larger cultural expectation of staying strong and not showing weakness. Whatever the reason, I was trying to force my way through without giving any space to actually feel and understand what was happening inside me. The idea of easing my foot off the gas so I could take care of myself was not an option I was willing to entertain. All I heard from myself was:

"You are the pastor . . . your church needs you."

"This is your job . . . you need to keep going and giving."

"Shake it off. Don't let the losses bother you."

"Why are you so tired? There are plenty of people who work more hours than you."

Each morning I would wake up exhausted. I'd sleep through the night and still not feel rested. This was a sign that something was off. Something within me needed to be tended to, but I kept pushing forward. Wondering when this weight would lift and I could get back to how it was before.

But, there was no going back. I was changing. My experiences were affecting me at a deep level. And trying to go back without addressing what I was feeling would only leave me spinning my tires. Stuck in the same place with all the exhaustion, disappointment, and grief I was carrying within.

In seminary, I had a professor who spoke often about the power of rituals. He saw them as a lost art in need of reclaiming. They were a way to viscerally experience milestones, rites of passage, and other moments of transition—the ones that brought joy and the ones that caused pain. By taking part in a ritual, you were getting out of your head and feeling your way through an experience.

Funerals were one of the rituals he would constantly talk about because they provide a space for grieving. We hold funerals for loved ones as a way to collectively grieve, laugh at memories, and mark the end of our physical time with a friend or family member. Funerals serve as a painful acknowledgment that what was before is not returning. It's the end of a season.

But the physical death of loved ones is not the only loss we experience. Life is an endless series of losses. Seasons are constantly changing. That which we value in one moment is no longer there the next.

Relationships.

A move away from the known.

Physical health.

A life stage.

Dreams for the future.

Rather than continuing to push aside what I was feeling, I needed to hold a funeral for what had been lost. The only way out of this season was through it. By being present to everything I was carrying within. To be honest with my grief and acknowledge it for what it was. Yes, it hurt when people walked away from what I'd created. Yes, it made me want to shrink back and give only when the result I desired was a guarantee.

This also meant taking care of myself as anyone going through a time of grieving should do. I shouldn't expect to be at the top of my game. Nor should I expect my energy or passion to be where it had been months earlier. Extending grace to myself was not something I was good at. But it was necessary if I was to ever regain that spark.

Mixed into the weariness and grief were a host of emotions connected to the upcoming birth of our first child. In just a month's time my life was about to radically change. Not knowing what to expect or what it would be like to become a father produced its own set of anxieties. It all felt like a roller coaster. One moment I'd be up, excited about my imminent role as parent. The next I'd be down, wishing I could leave the church to pursue work that required less of my soul. I was having trouble knowing what to do with this wide mix of feelings and emotions.

Finding people whose only agenda for us is that we would become the best, most alive version of ourselves is difficult. Too often, I find myself walking away from a conversation wondering if I was being encouraged to walk my path or the one someone else thought I should be walking. It's an unsettling feeling, as if someone is placing their agenda on you instead of helping you discover the right step for you. I'm fortunate to have people in my life with no agenda other than seeing me thrive. Rob has been that in my life. His voice was a refreshing sound in the midst of all the others in my head telling me to keep pushing, avoiding the reality of what I was feeling.

He was modeling the Eucharist way of living that I was continually being invited to follow. A place where expectations are set aside. Where you are simply free to give of yourself to others. You aren't giving because of what you'll get in return. It's not so others will fall in line behind you, boosting your ego. You're giving because it brings joy. You deeply care about others but don't need (or expect) anything in return.

The way of Eucharist goes against how much of our world works. We're transactional beings. Freely receiving can make us uncomfortable. We feel indebted. Initially, I felt I owed Rob something for having received "the bro rate." I'm used to paying for what I receive.

It was this transactional way of viewing my work that was stealing life from me. I wasn't receiving that which I believed

I deserved for the time, effort, and love I had given. And that gap in expectations was beginning to sow seeds of bitterness in my heart, leaving me exhausted.

The better way is the way of Eucharist. But before I could get there, I had to refill my soul. I had to allow myself to receive rest, grace, and renewed joy so I would have something to offer others, regardless of the outcome.

Unfortunately, I'd been running on empty for too long, and my son was about to be born, providing a whole new set of experiences to navigate through.

Burnout

It all came crashing down. Things had been moving in this direction for a while. I just didn't have enough awareness to see how burned out I was. And, despite the advice Rob had given me earlier, I didn't allow myself the space and time my soul needed. I hadn't explored the growing resentment I held within.

I'd been putting so much pressure on myself and my wife to keep the church going. We felt we were the glue that held everyone together, but as the church started to grow, this became impossible. There were too many people we felt responsible for.

It doesn't mean we didn't try.

In the early days of the church, we hosted a group at our house every week. We gathered together for discussion and dinner. Later, we shifted to hosting twice a month, still serving dinner each time. And when I say dinner, I mean *dinner*. A hot, home-cooked meal complete with vegetables and side dishes.

The group was growing. Most weeks we'd have more than twenty people in our house; we had to set up extra tables and chairs so everyone could sit and eat. People contributed by bringing dinner some weeks, but the weight of hosting began weighing us down. After a time, it became something we did because it was my job. The initial joy was gone.

One night, Steph and I were invited to the apartment of a couple who had just started attending the church. It was our third "interview" with them while they figured out who we were and if Awaken met their belief criteria. Earlier that week, I had started a sermon series on the story of Noah and the flood. Right out of the gate, they asked if I believed the story happened as it's written. When I introduced the story in church, I'd invited everyone to set aside whether the story was literal or not because, if we became caught up there, all our energy would be invested in proving or disproving the story rather than discovering the truths it held for us today. I guess that didn't go over well.

There I was, literally backed into a corner of their apartment, being asked if I thought a story from thousands of years ago happened exactly as it was described.

Driving home that night, Steph and I were upset thinking about everything else we could have been doing with our time. Instead, we spent the night being grilled by a couple who later that week told us they were leaving. They didn't think Awaken was a church they could bring friends to because they wouldn't be given a firm foundation of Christian beliefs.

That one stung.

We were overextending ourselves.

Trying to make everyone happy.

Forgoing healthy boundaries for the sake of the cause.

And it was slowly stealing our energy, passion, and joy.

I wish I'd listened to that intuition earlier in the year that had told me to slow down.

To rest.

Set some healthy boundaries between church and personal life.

Prepare myself for what was to come.

Instead, I kept pushing on.

Then, our son, Reece, was born.

Shortly after his birth, Steph herniated a disc, making her recovery from a C-section that much more difficult. We also learned why Reece was waking up every two to three hours each night. He was colicky—a word I later discovered sends shivers up the spine of many parents whose children have suffered through this. This all meant my sleep quantity and quality were non-existent. No matter how much caffeine I pumped into my veins, I spent my days sleepwalking.

On top of caring for my wife and newborn son, I still felt like I had a church to carry on my shoulders. I was the one responsible for its success. I was the one everyone was relying on. There were sermons to give and people to meet with. Having lost some members that year, I placed extra pressure on myself to replace those who'd left and make sure no one else walked out the door.

I had to keep going.

I knew I had little to offer, but I'd planned to take two weeks off when Reece was born. Any more time away would be a sign of defeat. It was guilt and fear that kept me going. Guilt about stopping and having to admit I didn't have it all together. Fear of losing this church that I had been pouring myself into for years. I still hadn't broken free of this fear-based way of living.

It took me a long time to get to the place where I finally shut it all down. About a month into Reece's life, he developed a fever on a Saturday afternoon which forced us to make a trip to the children's hospital.

That night is forever seared into my memory.

One of the first things the doctors did was insert a long needle into his spine. Just hearing they were going to do this to our one-month-old son was bad enough, but then they dropped the news that neither Steph nor I would be allowed in the room when it happened. We were left helplessly waiting in an examination room while he was wheeled away by strangers in a mobile steel crib with jail-like bars on all four sides.

After that procedure, they wanted to keep him in overnight. He was so young and the doctors wanted to be sure the fever wasn't a sign of something serious. By the time we were finally admitted into a room, it was well past midnight. We were exhausted. I spent the night on a five-foot-long blue plastic cushioned couch with my feet dangling off the end, while Steph slept in a rollaway cot.

When the sun rose early the next morning, it was Sunday. Time for work. Time for me to open the church and deliver the glorious sermon I'd prepared for the week. It didn't matter that my son was in the hospital hooked up to an IV drip. I was going to be there on time, ready to go. I was the pastor. The glue. The one who always showed a strong exterior because of my unwavering faith and commitment. So I rushed home, took a shower, brewed a big pot of coffee, and delivered my sermon.

I'm telling you this story because it pretty much sums up how that year went. It felt like one setback after the next while trying to appear unshaken. I had spent so long holding it together, denying my exhaustion . . . until early October when I started noticing some health problems and made an appointment to see a doctor.

As I sat on the examination table, she asked, "Are you experiencing any stress in your life?"

Well, that question opened the valve. She had given me space to let my guard down and I jumped in. I started talking and didn't stop.

I told her about the colic.

The herniated disc.

The sleepless nights.

The trip to the hospital.

I told her how I felt like I had to hold everything together at church for fear of it falling apart.

She sat on her black stool, calmly listening to all of it. After I was finished, she told me what I was experiencing health-wise was most likely stress related. She suggested I take some time off and find a therapist whom I could talk with about all I was going through.

After leaving her office, walking through the parking lot on that crisp October morning, I decided to take her advice.

I finally stopped running from what I knew I had to do.

For myself.

My family.

The church.

Before even leaving the parking lot, I started making phone calls to line up guest speakers for the next few weeks. I called the church board to tell them I had to take some time off. I found a therapist and set up my first appointment which proved to be easy with a blank calendar. Then I went home and took a nap.

Making that decision felt like a weight had lifted. There was no pressure hanging over me to duct-tape something together for a sermon each week. No leadership decisions to make. No phone calls to check in on how people were doing. I was free of all responsibilities.

That feeling lasted a little over two weeks. Then the anxiety started creeping back. I can see it in this next email. There's this unhealthy, relentless drive to get back to work. A few weeks off was OK, but now I was feeling the pressure to return. People were going to start wondering what was going on!

From: **Dave Stradling**
  To: Rob Bell
Date: October 23, 2017

Hey Rob!

I hit a spot of burnout the other week and had to take some unplanned time off. My level of stress was through the roof and I've been ignoring it for a while.

Just the thought of having to put a sermon together was paralyzing.

I've had three weeks off and have two more planned to not speak, but how do I know when I'm ready to speak again? During these few weeks, I've had no desire to put anything together and even started feeling that I don't care if I ever speak again. Today is the first day where I'm starting to feel a small spark of caring and wanting to actually keep going. I'm trying to put myself back together during this time; I've started seeing a therapist and am trying to learn to live differently.

I know deep within that I want to keep going, but also know there's some resentment and anger that I need to keep working through in order to recapture my joy. I'm having a tough time wrestling through the "I should get back/the church needs me/this might fall apart if I don't come back" vs. "I need to get healthy." How do I know when I am ready to go back?

Thanks!

Dave

From: **Rob Bell**
　To:　Dave Stradling
Date:　October 23, 2017

dude, relax. this might take a while.
and that's fine.

if the church falls apart while you're gone,
then it wasn't a church in the first place, right?
you're probably most angry with yourself for
not having better boundaries. at least that's
what i've seen the most. take your time.

whatever you do, don't set the return date.
that will cause your anxiety to spike like crazy.
and here's the thing: you'll know when you're
ready. i've had a few serious burnouts where
i couldn't speak. it took a while. and then one
day you wake up and you're ready. but you
can't rush it. and nothing crushes the soul more
than giving it a date on which it must be healed.
you're going to be fine.
give me a shout whenever you need to be reminded!

From: **Dave Stradling**
   To: Rob Bell
Date: October 24, 2017

Thank you.

I don't need any more anxiety—that's what got me
into this mess; trying to control everything and
overextending myself to ensure the outcome I wanted
which rarely worked.

I've been gripping everything so tightly and I don't want to do that anymore. I can't do that anymore.

Thanks for the permission to let my soul rest.

Rob's response calmed my growing anxiety. "Don't set the return date." So I didn't. I trusted that I'd know when I was ready to speak again.

On Sunday mornings, I would sit outside our house on a rocking chair, waving as my wife and son drove off to church. I'd lost all energy to care. In reality, I'd lost that energy long ago, only now I had been given permission to not care. For the first time since the start of the church, I was letting go.

I used those weeks to get myself healthy and didn't give any thought to when I'd be back. I spent more time with my family. I read for the joy of reading instead of needing sermon material, finally trading my incessant drive to slog through Wallace's *Infinite Jest* for the more appropriate Jack Reacher series. I exercised. I took a trip to Nashville with a good friend. It was exactly what I needed.

Eventually, I made my way back to church. It felt odd being a spectator in something I had started. Others had taken my place. I saw the church could go on without me. The pressure I had been placing on myself to be and do everything was unnecessary. No one expected that of me. It wasn't my job to be the glue that held it all together. I had so many good friends who believed in the church and wanted to see it succeed as much as I did. By attempting to carry the weight of it by myself, I was preventing them from giving their gifts to this community we had formed together.

My forced time of retreat was changing me. I was beginning to see things I hadn't noticed earlier that were draining my energy and taking me away from the life I truly desired to live. Habits. Mindsets. Beliefs. In the mornings, I started sitting at my desk, taking notes on all I was learning. Quickly, the pages filled up with all that was flowing out of me.

As the weeks passed, I found myself restless when sitting in church listening to someone else speak. I wanted to be the one up there. I had ideas I wanted to share. I came up with a series of sermons connecting the story of Christmas with all I was experiencing called "The Advent of Disruption." No extra studying was necessary. I didn't have to crack a single book. It was all there inside me.

The old spark was coming back. And with it came glimpses of:

desire

passion

excitement

joy.

I was ready.

Relearning How to Live

Monday, December 4, 2017

My first Sunday back was pure joy! I had a message I couldn't wait to give. These ideas had been bubbling up inside me for weeks, and I had to share them. All the anxiety of not having anything to say, or wondering if I ever would again, was gone. The lack of desire to give a sermon was replaced with an excitement to give others a glimpse into what was changing in me. At that point, it was the most true-to-me sermon I had ever given. It flowed right out of me.

After I'd finished, a woman who had been standing at the back came forward and thanked me for taking time off. "You showed us it's OK to not be OK. If even the pastor can say, 'I need help,' then all of us are able to do that in our lives."

I never saw this before her comment, but my time off was an embodied sermon in itself. It wasn't an idea being communicated verbally. It was a truth being lived out in my life, fully on display for all to see. I was coming to know the truth by how I was living and, in turn, inviting others to do the same.

Prior learnings were embedding themselves deeper into my being. More and more I was seeing how my life truly is the message. And, as painful as it was, I am thankful for that time. It taught me lessons I would never have learned any other way. Those months revealed how much in my life needed to change if I wanted to walk a path free from the unhealthy pressure and expectations I had been placing on myself.

In our first meeting, my therapist made an interesting observation. He suggested I was shadow-boxing myself—running around a ring, throwing punches at an imaginary opponent. I believed I was defending myself by trying to hold my ground. But in reality, there was no one else in the ring with me. My energy was being exhausted by an imaginary fight, mostly with my own expectations.

When I became a pastor, I unknowingly created a set of expectations about who I was supposed to be. They were the rules I lived by:

- How I was supposed to schedule my time.

- When I was supposed to be available for people.

- What I was supposed to say in my sermons.

- What I wasn't supposed to say in my sermons.

- How often I was supposed to meet with those who attended church.

- The questions I was supposed to ask in conversations.

- The topics I was supposed to talk about.

- The beliefs I was supposed to hold.

- How many times I was supposed to pray in meetings.

No one created these expectations for me. I had started this church which meant there were no expectations carried over from a former pastor. I was free to define how I would operate.

Yet here I was, boxing myself in. And it wasn't working. I wasn't being true to *me*. To the unique path the Spirit was leading me on.

This season began the process of setting myself free. I was in the early stages of understanding how these expectations were affecting me, but I look back and see this as a turning point. I realized I couldn't continue in the same way I'd been going before my time off. If I was going to continue speaking and leading a church, I had to learn to operate differently.

From: **Dave Stradling**
  To: Rob Bell
Date: December 4, 2017

Hey Rob,

I spoke yesterday for the first time in over two months and it felt great! I really do feel like a different person— more confident and ready to embrace this work. I think a lot of the stress was the internal pressure of expectations and trying to be someone who others wanted me to be up there. I was trying to control all the outcomes and that was creating all sorts of anxiety. It's almost as if the burnout was a gift to begin breaking a lot of that within me. I know I still have work to do but am feeling back on track.

During those weeks before I stopped speaking, it felt like I had nothing to say and I was scrambling to put something together. Now I feel like I have way more to say and am feeling alive again preparing and giving a sermon!

As I ease my way back into this, do you have any suggestions of what I should be paying attention to so I don't find myself in the same place? I'm incorporating a whole new set of rhythms and practices like setting up my calendar further in advance, speaking fewer weeks in a row, and passing off other church responsibilities so I can focus more on being the healthiest I can be for myself, my family, and the church.

Thanks!

Dave

From: **Rob Bell**
  To: Dave Stradling
Date: December 5, 2017

oh man, i am high-fiving the universe with you!!!
i totally know the feeling: you once wondered if you'd
ever do it again because you had nothing to say. so
you throw it all up in the air and walk away to get
healthy and then it comes back a thousand times
more fun and loose and dangerous and joyous than
ever because you've had it taken away.

SO YOU'RE ACTUALLY ABLE TO SEE IT FOR THE
GIFT THAT IT WAS THE WHOLE TIME.

first, show your wife all your scheduling. let her
give green and red lights.
actually, take it farther, ask three or four people
you trust and LOVE to hang out with you. if you can,
buy them lunch once a month for the next few
months. show them a pie chart of how you've been
spending your time. show them your calendar from
the previous month. ask them what they think. you'll
be blown away with the wisdom they have just looking
at things, they'll see things you never would have thought
of. when i did this, i was shocked at how my group kept
saying "too much! too much! not enough rest and play
time!" get those voices speaking in your head to help
push out those old anxious voices.

second, you have energy now. that is not energy to go
back and do a thousand things. that's energy for your
family, for fitness and play and curiosity and all the things
you didn't do before because you were saving the world.
make sense? your first impulse may be to take all this
new energy and give it right back to the black hole that sucked
it all away in the first place.
no.
give it to having a life. because
THAT'S WHERE THE SERMONS COME FROM.

trust that.
that if you're wide awake to life—
getting the oil changed, pushing your kid in a stroller,
buying carpet, going to ship something at UPS—when
you're awake and present and not
anxious and cooked
then in those everyday interactions you'll be picking
up a world of stories and wisdom and insight and
connections.

you will have more to say than you ever thought imaginable.
but it won't come from working more
or studying more—
it will come from
living
deeper.
make sense?

From: **Dave Stradling**
   To: Rob Bell
 Date: December 6, 2017

Yes, that all makes sense! I haven't been enjoying
life because of everything else I was spending my
time doing.

For a while I've been feeling this pull toward a different way of living and I am going to trust that and learn a whole new way of creating and living life.

I don't know where that's going to lead, but I know I can't go back to how it was.

And yes, I talked a bit about these past few months on Sunday. A few people came up to me after, saying they were sorry for what I'd been going through. But even as they were saying that, I knew I had to go through everything in order to get here, so painful but freeing at the same time.

Once the adrenaline-fueled high of speaking that first Sunday wore off, I was still left with a bout of depression. The mysterious health issues hadn't disappeared. I had expected everything to be resolved by resting. When that didn't happen, I was disappointed. I was doing all the right things by prioritizing health, minimizing stress, learning to set better boundaries, and talking with a therapist, but I wasn't seeing the results I'd hoped for.

The next few months were difficult as my mood swung like a pendulum. One minute I'd be hopeful, trying a new health fix—juicing celery, special diets, supplements, alternative medical practices—only to have those hopes crushed when the expected result didn't materialize.

While I was back to giving sermons, I wasn't experiencing life in a deeper way than before. I was so fixated on finding answers to these health challenges that I was missing the life in front of me.

Finally, one night in April, I couldn't sleep. In the middle of the night, I was lying in bed, thinking. I'd shut everything down because I wanted to live from a place of joy. Yet, it mostly felt like I wasn't making any progress in that direction. I had so much in front of me—family, friends, job, health—but I wasn't allowing myself to enjoy any of it. All my attention was focused on resolving a non-life-threatening health condition which I was successfully learning how to manage.

That night was another one of those moments forever etched in my memory. I'd reached the bottom. In that moment, my feeble prayer was that I would no longer live trying to control everything. I had been doing that with the church; now I was doing the same with my health.

I wanted to be free to pursue joy. I wanted to be wide awake to life. Enjoying all the goodness present before me. I wanted my energy to go toward creating a life rather than having it consumed by a constant preoccupation with all that wasn't going how I expected. Lying there that night, I made a vow to give myself to the pursuit of joy. With each step I took toward this new life, the fog slowly started lifting.

2018 became a year of recovery. A year of relearning how to live.

I took a full inventory of how I was spending my time. Learning to say no was something I slowly became better at. As a young pastor, I'd been given the advice to always say yes to others' requests. Following this advice often left me angry for not having the grit to say no when I knew it wasn't right for me.

Other times, I would spend hours trying to find a good excuse for saying no. Steph and I would go back and forth debating if the excuse would be "good enough." You know you're in trouble when it's gotten to that level! I've now learned you don't need a "good excuse" for why you can't be somewhere. Sometimes it's just a no.

I began discarding the earlier wisdom offered to me and became more selective about what I said yes to. This meant no more evening interviews about my beliefs. No more hosting a meal for twenty people every other week. I had a young family at home and that dynamic alone changed how I organized my time. It was a new season. As with any new season, scheduling, boundaries, and expectations have to be adjusted. It's been a continuous journey of learning what works for us.

My burnout also helped me come to terms with the truth of limitations. I am finite. I can't do everything. Nor should I try. I am here to offer the best of myself to this world. Living with no limitations, trying to be everything, was leaving me with little energy to give to this pursuit. I wasn't taking care of myself and my body knew it. For months, it had been communicating this truth, but I'd stubbornly refused to listen. I kept trying to be more than who I was as I attempted to live up to the expectations of who I thought others wanted me to be.

All that began to break during this season. I started seeing the importance of protecting myself. Guarding my life and the gifts I had to offer the world. As I learned to do so, I became free to pursue the truest version of me. No longer did I have to be pulled in different directions. I could shape my life in a way that cultivated the best of what I had to offer.

Steph and I took time for ourselves, figuring out how to be in this new space of parenting. Evaluating each new season, doing our best to protect ourselves and ensure we didn't return to our previous ways of living. We relearned how to lead a church without having it all rely on us, but allowing others an opportunity to carry the weight.

I allowed myself more time to rest, revisiting old practices that had once filled me with life. Weekly walks in the woods. Matinee movies in the theater. Consistent trips to the gym. Regular time with friends.

I picked up new practices like Tuesday morning yoga class. I began paying close attention to my energy levels, taking more Sundays off from speaking as I noticed how many weeks I could go before losing the joy of it.

I also invited friends on this journey. Friends I had known for years, who loved and believed in me. They asked questions which helped me discern what to pursue and when to say no. They encouraged me to give time to projects that were energizing. Their only agenda was to see me follow the unique passions and gifts I possessed within.

Ever so slowly, the old mindset began to fade away and was replaced with a new enthusiasm for life. An excitement to continue growing in the art of communicating.

In many ways, 2018 was a difficult year. The exhaustion took a long time to work itself out of my bones. Even to this day, Steph and I talk about the toll those first few years of starting a church took on us. The unrelenting pressure we placed on ourselves for the success and growth of the church. We're still seeing how deeply those years affected us.

If it weren't for this season, who knows how much longer we would have gone on living with the pressure? Those expectations I'd created would only have become more intertwined with my identity. The gift of this season is one I will forever be grateful for as it taught me I could live free of those burdens.

Sermons as Comedy Bits

I was in the middle of a sermon series on Colossians when I wrote this next email. Fresh from my time off, I'd started preparing in January. A few people had recently recommended a commentary on Colossians and I was intrigued to learn more about this ancient letter.

Soon, I reverted to old habits. The books piled up. Every insight led me down another trail with more information to dig up. As the weeks went by, I was feeling the weight of needing to have my sermons ready to go. I was seeing so much and making so many connections, there wasn't enough time to learn everything. I was still expecting myself to be the authority on a given subject. I was still hoping to blow people away with all the connections I could make between this ancient letter and our modern world.

This way of thinking was returning me to the path of exhaustion. I was running on a never-ending treadmill.

From: **Dave Stradling**
 To: Rob Bell
Date: April 30, 2018

Hi Rob!

I'm still working on finding the right balance between too much detail and not enough detail in my sermon outlines. I've noticed that when I don't have enough of an outline, I tend to be less focused and repeat myself more. Yet, having too much detail makes me less free because I'm trying to remember way too many things.

Am I still trying to pack too much into a sermon? Making things too complex? Could it be a mental thing where I am putting too much pressure on myself? I'm convinced my health problems started from gripping everything (including sermon work) too tightly. I still feel like I am doing too much memorizing and it's paralyzing my brain when I'm up there.

Thanks!

Dave

———

From: **Rob Bell**
 To: Dave Stradling
Date: May 2, 2018

let's do this . . .

> I'm still working on finding the right balance between too much detail and not enough detail in my sermon outlines.

*this is a totally normal question! and this is
exactly what happens when you get serious
about the craft. you start paying attention
to all the subtle parts—like the bulk or slimness
of your outline. welcome to the art form! haha*

> I've noticed that when I don't have enough of an outline, I tend to be less focused and repeat myself more. Yet, having too much detail makes me less free because I'm trying to remember way too many things.

*try switching up your outline, here's a few thoughts:
this week, put your outline up on the screen so everybody
can see it, and then walk them through your outline for the
sermon. here's the thing: they'll love it. you'll be shocked at
how much love and connection it brings.*

*you've been performing, trying to do good work for them,
but what they really want is someone to show them all of it—
the parts where you're still figuring it out, all the ways that you
are learning how to do good work.*

*because in showing them how you're learning and growing
and giving yourself to better communication,
you're teaching them how to give themselves to THEIR work …
get it?*

so as you're doing the sermon, give them running commentary
on what you left in and what you edited out
and why you made those choices . . .
turn the sermon into a workshop on . . .
sermons . . .

remember, if you've lived with it for years and
months and weeks,
and you can't remember it,
how will they ever?

| Am I still trying to pack too much into a sermon?

yes. if you're asking, you are.
this was what i did for years.
i was driven by breath.
how much i could show them i knew.
i would show them 20 bible verses in a sermon,
almost like i was validating my paycheck.
but as you get older and wiser you'll find
depth
much more interesting.

| Making things too complex?

yep, slow it down.
relax.
live with the sermon and let it breathe.

> I still feel like I am doing too much memorizing and
> it's paralyzing my brain when I'm up there.

so let's experiment with different kinds of outlines.
i already suggested showing them the outline so it's up
on the screen.
you'll be amazed how much this frees you.
another thing is to get big sheets of paper and write the outline
out and then put the sheets on the floor so you only
have to look down at the floor.

and tell them.
tell them you're trying something new.
see where i'm going with this?
you've been trying to give them a fantastic spiritual show,
which is fine,
but here's the next step for you:
to turn the attempt to give a good sermon into the sermon.
you with me?
stop hiding it from them,
let them in . . .
let them see you trying new things.
let them see you figuring it out.

do you see what this does?
this rescues you from your fear.
if it bombs, then the sermon becomes about how to keep
your cool when you bomb.
right?

*so many preachers are trying to avoid the very things
that help people—YOU BEING HUMAN AND GIVING YOURSELF
TO YOUR WORK WITHOUT FEAR AND WITH JOY AND FREEDOM.*

*breathe deeper,
relax,
there's nothing that can go wrong here
except
you not being open to whatever might go wrong
and rolling with it with grace and humor and love.*

*if you forget your place,
stop and look at your notes.
and tell them you got so excited you forgot what was next.
if you're cramming too much in,
edit it out on the spot
and tell them there's only one thing you want them to hear
that day.*

*see what i mean?
turn the sermon into what's happening in and through you in
that moment . . .*

what do you think?

From: **Dave Stradling**
To: Rob Bell
Date: May 3, 2018

Yes—this explains a lot; I HAVE been trying to perform and put on a spiritual show.

And all that pressure I've been putting on myself to perform has been making the entire process less enjoyable, which I'm sure is less life-giving for everyone.

I keep wanting to be somewhere down the line, rather than allowing myself to be where I am in this moment.

I keep wishing I was ten steps further.

One of my biggest frustrations has been knowing something is true but then preparing and speaking about it has made me see that I'm not as deep into that belief/idea as I thought and there's more depth to explore. Trying to be further along is making me feel unintegrated because my wisdom hasn't caught up to my knowledge. I'm guessing the thing for me to do would be relax and just teach the idea from the place where I'm at instead of coming across as the expert.

Ha, you're right, I'm trying to avoid the messiness of growing into an idea. I'm expecting to be an expert on something which is why I've always wanted to read as much of the literature on a topic before I preach about it. But I know that's not wisdom, just intellectual knowledge. I was going to try putting together my next bunch of sermons with no more reading but just sitting with what's already within me.

Cool, I will put the outline on the screen this week and experiment with the big sheets in the next couple of weeks.

I'm loving discovering this craft; I just need to get out of my own way!

This helps a lot, thank you!

From: **Rob Bell**
  To: Dave Stradling
Date: May 3, 2018

well said
it's going to be so much more fun ...
remember,
you've sat with this for so long.
just tell them what's already in you,
that alone will blow people away
in a good way

After this latest email exchange, as I prepared for the next sermon series, I followed through with what I told Rob I would do. I put away all the books and sat with a pen and blank notebook, asking:

What have I been learning?

Where have I been experiencing the Spirit?

The next series was titled *Christmas in July (and August): Finding Peace and Joy.* I looked deeper within and crafted a series of sermons about how I was rediscovering peace and joy in my life.

It was so easy!

And fun.

The weight was gone.

I wasn't trying to be an authority on anything other than my life.

I started experimenting. Having fun. Learning to let go of giving "the perfect sermon."

Later that year, I told a friend that I saw myself as a stand-up comedian working out bits. I'd read about comedians who, before taking a show on the road, would find a small local comedy club where they could practice their routines. Some would bring a notebook on stage, taking notes in real time. They'd be paying attention to how the audience reacted, and make changes based on their response. Some jokes were cut out, others expanded, and some were completely altered.

These comics were experimenting. Learning their craft in front of a live audience. There was no fear of failure, no need to be perfect. They knew it wasn't going to be. They expected certain parts not to work how they envisioned. I'm sure the audience loved it. Imagine sitting in a small club watching Robin Williams try out a joke for the first time!

This way of practicing a craft is inspiring. It acknowledges that any form of art—and a sermon is just that—is never perfected. You're constantly growing.

One week, I put notes on the screen behind me. The next week, I made copies of my notes and handed them out before the sermon. I tried writing my notes on giant sheets of paper and placing them on the floor in front of me. Another time, I used props instead of written notes, each prop illustrating a different part of the sermon.

I was trying to see what worked best; what helped me feel the most free when I was speaking. Just the practice of trying these ideas was liberating. I began to see the sermon as a living, breathing experience instead of a flat, one-dimensional lecture during which I transferred information. It's taken four years, but I'm now trusting other approaches besides the information tool I was so reliant on when Rob first listened to a recording of my sermon.

A few weeks after this email, I was in the middle of a sermon when I completely lost my place. My mind went blank. I'd forgotten where I was in my outline, and the slides weren't on the screen or anywhere in sight. I began to panic. I couldn't let them know! What would they think? But then, after taking a breath, I stopped and told everyone I'd lost my place. I had to check my notes because what I was saying was really important and I wanted to clearly communicate it. No one said a thing. In fact, one friend mentioned afterwards that it was his favorite sermon of the series.

That experience gave me more confidence. Confidence to laugh at myself and to lessen the paralyzing grip I was placing on my work. When you speak every week, it's inevitable that not everything will go according to plan. Those moments can derail the sermon. They can ruin the rest of my day as I fixate on what went wrong, or I can roll with it, using it all as sermon material.

A few years later, I was about to speak when my four-year-old son came rushing toward me. He was refusing to go into the kids' service, and Steph wasn't there to sit with him. So I did what any desperate parent would do in such a situation.

I bribed him.

It didn't work. He wanted to be with me and wouldn't take no for an answer.

Left with no choice, I found a stool and sat him on my lap. And then delivered my sermon.

He sat there the whole time. On my lap.

When I got home, I showed Steph the video. She was horrified. And impressed. Especially watching me tear open his bag of Goldfish crackers and flip the spout on his water bottle mid-sermon without missing a beat. Even more impressive, later that week, he started talking about Sabbath, the topic of my sermon that day.

Nothing can go wrong up there.

Unless, of course, I let it.

I started learning to let go of the performance. To let others see behind the curtain. For years I had hidden behind my intellect. Toiling to prove to others I was the expert. Now, I was discovering that's not what we want anyway. What we truly want is for others to share their life with us.

Discoveries made.

Workings of the Spirit.

The ups.

The downs.

Experiments that didn't work out.

Trails of curiosity followed.

Lessons learned from the moments it all blew up.

Honesty.

Vulnerability.

Questions still left unanswered.

Joy experienced.

Pain.

It took a forced season of vulnerability to realize this is what people are truly looking for. Not a spiritual show, but someone who opens up their life for others to see. Someone who has been paying close attention to their experiences and shows others how to do the same. This, after all, is where the Spirit is found. Right at the place we find ourselves. Not in ideas, but in the experience of life itself.

In the Gospel of John, when Jesus begins gathering followers, his initial invitation is to "come and see." (John 1:39). This was an invitation into experience. An invitation for others to witness something for themselves. Jesus was opening up his life. Trusting that, as he did so, others would have their own personal encounters with God.

When my son was in the hospital the previous year, my sermon made no mention of what was happening. I was trying to show a strong exterior. Why? What was I trying to prove? Why hadn't I talked about the uncertainty and fear of what I was experiencing? The anger toward the situation? Why didn't I talk about the absence of God that I was feeling? I wasn't allowing myself to go there unless I'd already written it into the sermon's script.

My understanding of what it means to be a pastor continued to evolve. I'm not here to give people the answers by passing along information. I'm to model a way of living. My role is to pay close attention to what's happening within and around me, then show what I'm seeing and point out what I've found to be true. By doing so, I'm showing others how to grow in their awareness. I'm inviting them to make their own discoveries and experience truth in their own lives.

This is an idea I'd seen years earlier, but was only now coming to trust. A staged performance would never allow for this way of being. I had to pull back the curtain.

Learning to Float

There are many qualities that make for a good teacher. One is knowing when a student is ready to take the next step. Ready to peel back another layer of truth.

After seeing me hit rock bottom and now learning to rebuild and create a sustainable life, Rob knew I was ready to go further. Sitting in my inbox one spring afternoon was an opportunity for me to keep traveling deeper into what I'd been discovering.

From: **Rob Bell**
To: Dave Stradling
Date: May 23, 2018

my man, an assignment for you:
martha beck
wrote a book called

finding your way in a wild new world.
part 1 is about wordlessness.
read it
report back
cool?

From: **Dave Stradling**
   To: Rob Bell
Date: May 30, 2018

Hey Rob!

I had a chance to read the section on wordlessness.

So much in there on so many levels.

She talked about how, in the past, a healer would first ask "when you stopped experiencing spontaneous joy." That idea really struck me because I'm realizing that I've allowed the joy to be taken out of my work and my life in general, and it's all from overthinking. She says truth is something you live, not something you think.

You've really hammered this one home for me. Whenever I am speaking from the truth that I have lived, it flows. I can feel it when I'm writing a sermon. If I feel stuck, I know it's because I'm outside the realm of truth that I've experienced. Unfortunately, I don't pick up on this quickly enough sometimes as it hasn't become normal for me yet. Whenever I'm overwhelmed or stressed, instead of feeling, I revert to thinking. But as I was going through the book, I tried some of the practices she recommended and I could feel a shift in me.

I feel as if I've forgotten how to play because I've become more concerned with having all the right answers and being at a particular point of the journey instead of enjoying the ride and being OK with where I am. I want to solve all the paradoxes, have an immediate answer for everything, and live with no uncertainty! Ha, I guess I like being the answer man. Is this why I find myself getting upset with people who see things as black and white? Because I have paradoxes sitting within me and I'm not OK with that??

There was so much in there that I already "knew" and she just put words to it. She talked about surrendering to fatigue—I've been conditioned to ignore fatigue and keep pressing forward! I know I need to listen to my body more and trust what it's telling me. I've known within me that I need more silence and nature in my life and yet I haven't carved out the space for it. I'm still in the "do" mode and this is showing me that I need time for both. Is it a bad thing to schedule time for it? Is this how I have to start so that I train my brain and become able to unconsciously switch back and forth as I go through the day?

A quote that really stood out to me is from the *Tao Te Ching*: "That which knows doesn't speak, that which speaks doesn't know." Yes! My job as a speaker is to show people, not tell them. And I have to be silent with it for a while so I can experience it, digest it, and then show it in a picture/ story/illustration. I think I struggle with putting a message together sometimes because I shouldn't be speaking on it yet! Crafting sermons really comes down to experiencing and then putting the books away so I can feel my way through it without words and then come back around to using words. And all I'm doing is witnessing to what I know to be truth which will most likely make me ramble less because I KNOW what I'm talking about.

How do I balance the input with the silence? I remember you mentioning input (books, magazines, etc.) is what sparks creativity. So am I reading a lot still but not with the intent of using that material for current sermons I'm working on?

I am excited! I feel this is the fun part of working this craft and making it my own!

Dave

My thoughts on Martha Beck's book included insights I'd been seeing for a few months and a slew of follow-up questions. Rob didn't answer those questions. He replied with another assignment.

From: **Rob Bell**
To: Dave Stradling
Date: May 31, 2018

you see why so many pastors—ok, people—end up
getting stuck, right?
they fail to ask the sorts of questions you're asking and then
they don't follow this where it leads
but you

you're on it
and that's fantastic
so let's try something, shall we?
try this for a week and tell me what happens:
try scheduling pastor/church things only from noon on,
and after you're with your family in the morning or whatever
you normally do, ask the question:
what would most feed my soul?
and then do that
read, hike, workout, walk

two things:

first, during that morning, if you have something from work
or the to-do list come to mind, jot it down, and then forget it—
you'll deal with it later.

second, any ideas you have, insights, stories, memories,
anything that you find interesting that comes across your
bow—note it.
keep those two things separate—
maybe the work/to-do etc list starts at the front of the notebook,
the other notes start at the back,
and then at or after lunch go back into your life
no emails, phone calls, meetings before noon
try it for a week
let's see what happens . . .
good?

From: **Dave Stradling**
  To: Rob Bell
Date: June 7, 2018

Hi Rob!

I went this whole week without doing any church work until after lunch. First, only checking email once a day was amazing! Definitely a practice that I will continue. Just being away from my computer and having my phone turned off for a good portion of the day has been very freeing.

I noticed a bunch of things:

Being outside fills me.

I felt like the day moved slower and was fuller; each day had more depth to it.

I was more focused and productive when I sat down to work. Sermon writing flowed more smoothly.

I was happier overall and more able to deal with frustration.

Being in an office for a whole day doesn't do it for me.

I found myself observing more details and people more closely.

I have the power/ability to create the life I want, and I haven't been doing a great job creating that life, which is so important for speaking.

As I was out walking/biking/reading, sermon material came much more easily than sitting at a desk. I see the necessity for study but am learning that the ideas and stories come as I let my mind go where it wants to go. Places where I was stuck became clear when I wasn't sitting at a desk, forcing something into existence.

Taking the time to fill my soul felt like I was creating space to let myself breathe. I've been operating out of the idea that "putting in my time" is what matters, but it's the depth that matters more and I've been suffocating some of that breath.

I haven't been giving myself permission to enjoy! This was a big one that came to me this morning. By not doing this, I am tightening everything and constricting the flow of the Spirit.

I noticed that when you get serious about your health/ work/etc., distractions always pop up. I am the one responsible for keeping myself healthy. No one else can do that for me.

I have way more work to do before wordlessness becomes more normal for me. I found my rational brain trying to take over quite a bit and still think my way through situations/problems.

How do I balance this way of living with pastor work? I'm lucky that I started this church so I can call the shots pertaining to my schedule. There's no set role of what a pastor looks like, which gives me freedom! Am I continuing to be so in tune with my soul that I know what my soul needs and then adjust my schedule accordingly?

Even scheduling days or mornings in advance so that I can stay vibrant and full? Is filling my soul and inputting ideas part of "the work"? It felt like my mornings were part of the work of being a healthier speaker/pastor. Is that my whole work? Filling myself so I have something to give? I'm guessing every season will look different, but me being inspired and joyful would definitely make me better for the people I pastor.

And then where is the separation between speaking life and not-speaking life?? One of the things I discovered is that I constantly found my mind working on upcoming sermons and ideas. Is that what this life looks like? How do I shut my teacher mind off so I am free to experience and learn myself?

I feel like all this is helping me be more human, which is the whole goal after all.

Thank you!

Dave

From: **Rob Bell**
  To: Dave Stradling
Date: June 8, 2018

this is great what you're doing here—
a few responses

> So how do I balance this way of living with pastor work?

if your marriage is falling apart, that has direct significance for your job, correct? so it's important to remember that part of this job is being you. it's fairly ambiguous at times— so your question is a great one. it's murky how it works. but what we do know is that you're no good to anyone if you're cooked. so central to you being you is you having a full tank.

> I'm lucky in that I started this church so I can call the shots pertaining to my schedule.

so yes, you call the shots. set it up how it works for you.

> Am I continuing to be so in tune with my soul that I know what my soul needs and then adjust my schedule accordingly?

yep. and people will respect this. because when you are engaged, when you're doing the work, you'll have a vitality and life that will actually help people.

> Even scheduling days or mornings in advance so that I can stay vibrant and full? Is filling my soul and inputting ideas part of "the work"?

again, yes!!

> I'm guessing every season will look different, but me being inspired and joyful would definitely make me better for the people I pastor.

then the question is: how do i set things up for this season? you'll be constantly tweaking things here on out. so think of it

in terms of seasons. constant conversation with your wife about what works for her, what you're dreaming of doing, what vision of the next year would thrill you both.
you get to figure this out.

> And then where is the separation between speaking life and not-speaking life?? One of the things I discovered is that I constantly found my mind working on upcoming sermons and ideas. is that what this life looks like?

remember, you're one week in. relax. your mind will calm down. you've been in a pattern where you have sunday panic, right? sunday is coming and you have to say something profound and your bucket is empty so it creates a low-grade tension all the time. you are one week in. imagine how you'll feel in a month. trust this process to calm you down, and fill your notebook.

> how do I shut my teacher mind off so I am free to experience and learn myself?

that will happen with time. imagine three months from now. you'll have so many ideas stockpiled, you'll be so much more rested and healthy. you'll literally be choosing which idea of the many to give a sermon on—you're building up muscles and that takes a bit.

if this feels radical, it is. most pastors don't live like this. they're stressed, burned-out messes. if this feels crazy it's because you're challenging an entire system of

workaholic insane culture that makes people miserable.
you're confronting it by quietly living a different way.
you've chosen not to be too busy. or distracted. you will
notice that as your energy is more calm and centered,
people will have questions. stay cool, and let your
presence do the work. simply witness to a deeper flow.
you'll be shocked at how the whole game changes . . .
you'll begin to see the insanity in others all around you.
you'll see how they're flying by amazing moments and
you're moving slower and you're seeing them . . .
stay with this,
report back. Hahaha

From: **Dave Stradling**
To: Rob Bell
Date: June 10, 2018

OK, great! This gives me a bunch to work on!

From the beginning, Rob wasn't just providing answers. He was offering tools to explore the questions on my own. There was always an invitation to practice something, then "report back." He was providing space for me to wrestle with all I was experiencing. A safe space. One of non-judgment and grace, no matter what feelings I expressed in my emails. And always a continued insistence to keep diving deeper. To keep feeding the fire of curiosity. It was in the questions where I would find my true self. They were a window through which I could peer into my soul.

In this email thread, I still see glimpses of my earlier anxiety to have it all figured out. It's taking time to jettison this way of thinking. But what I love most here is my trail of discovery. I'm going further, deeper, with all I'm learning. Things that come naturally to me now, I can look back on and see where I started growing into them.

There's an initial disbelief that I "was allowed" to set up my life in such a way. I'd been stuck for so long. Drowning in expectations about what a pastor is supposed to be like, I found it difficult to imagine any other way of living. I even managed to deflate my excitement by turning it all into another form of work. Something I had to tirelessly strive for.

From: **Rob Bell**
  To: Dave Stradling
Date: June 10, 2018

well, david, i think you're ready for the real
truth, the truth behind the truth:
ready?
(how's that for build up)
it's not about work.
it's about flow.

here's what i mean: as we start to wake up,
it's easy for us to beat ourselves up for all the
ways we've missed out or been blind or ignorant,
etc etc.

we're fighters and so we resolve to work harder
push harder, commit even more.
here's what i want you to think about:
think about dropping the idea of working on it.
it's not bad,
it's just that there are other ways of seeing it.

here's one: flow.
here's another one: joining.
here's another one: listening.

see what i mean?

a guy i knew years ago recently texted me and he
thanked me because he said i "never stop pushing ahead"
but here's the thing:
it doesn't feel like pushing.
it feels like floating down a river.

yes, there's obviously work in it,
but what i want you to think about is flow.
you're joining a flow.
no beating yourself up, no back-breaking effort,
no striving or grasping energy,
you listening for whatever the next step is for dave,
and then taking that next step.

you with me?

you're so smart and so hungry and so ready to go—
which is great, that's why I engage with you—
only some people are willing like you are!
but that can actually get in the way at times.

a whole new world is opening up for you,
so trust it and let it unfold
picture yourself floating down a river
let the current do the work.
you just float.
you with me?

From: **Dave Stradling**
To: Rob Bell
Date: June 12, 2018

Haha—yes, I am with you!

I know exactly what you're talking about and know that I've been fighting that flow at times because I haven't developed the confidence yet to trust where it's taking me.

Yes, I'm on board with developing the muscles to trust this new world and just float wherever it is taking me.

Thanks for helping me see this! I'll keep you updated!

Like so many of us, my life had been built on a foundation of doing. Doing helps us believe we are in control. By doing, we seek to prove ourselves. Show we are worthy. Receiving worth or value without working for it felt foreign to me. But that very effort prevented me from seeing this deeper life already flowing within and around me.

In previous emails, I spoke a few times of "intuitively" knowing what to do. Or feeling a pull in a certain direction. Even the questions I asked revealed a level of knowing. I knew the path to walk. There was an inner wisdom already at work within me, but I hadn't learned to fully trust it. In some moments, yes. But I was still largely seeking outside permission. My seeking and striving had been so externally focused, I couldn't see the wisdom already present within me.

The Bible has a lot to say about wisdom. According to the book of Proverbs, not only has wisdom been around from the beginning of creation, it is intertwined with creation itself. Without wisdom, there is no life.

Living by the wisdom present from the beginning is seen in the Bible as the highest pursuit. When you live by wisdom, you are living in alignment with the creation we are all a part of. We could call it "living in the flow of the universe." It's this way of living that brings life, while living out of the flow brings death. We all know this to be true.

Bitterness.

Hatred.

Revenge.

Greed.

These ways of living close our hearts and leave us feeling confined and empty.

Generosity.

Love.

Grace.

Forgiveness.

These ways of living leave us feeling free and alive.

The feelings we experience from such ways of being are our inner wisdom communicating to us. Showing us the path to life. The way to live as the truest version of ourselves. This inner wisdom is a gift. It's the divine Spirit within.

In my senior year of high school, our church took the graduating seniors camping on the Delaware River. After setting up camp the evening before, we woke early on a sunny Saturday morning. A bus drove us a few miles upstream where we boarded a raft and started our trip downriver. Much of the early spring runoff had slowed, so it was a calm trip. There were no large rapids to navigate.

The trip took most of the day, and we spent it laughing, eating food, and soaking up the sun. We were in no hurry. Every once in a while, we'd paddle to the shore for shade or to explore something that had caught our attention. Some spots had rocks we climbed and jumped off into the river below. Whenever the heat was too much, we'd flip off the raft and float next to it to cool off. Eventually, we made it back to our campsite, having exerted little effort in the journey downriver.

This wasn't a journey of speed.

It wasn't an anxious journey spent trying to direct the current.

We weren't left exhausted from attempting to paddle hard against the flow of the river.

It was a journey of trusting that the current would lead us in the right direction.

An unhurried journey with space to enjoy and explore whatever caught our attention.

This was a journey of open-eyed wonder. What hidden adventure lay around the next bend?

It was this way of understanding my life that I was now being invited into.

Trust.

Slowness.

Exploration.

Open-eyed wonder.

Moving with the larger flow I was already swimming in.

I'd seen the result of tirelessly working to control my path. I wanted no part of that. It was a dead end. But if there truly was a different way to live, I wanted in. If there was a way of letting go and being led into a larger, simpler, deeper, more joyous, and purpose-filled life, I was ready to embrace it. I was ready to grab my inner tube and see where the river would lead.

"Rest Now, Stressed-Out Pastor"

Tuesday, September 11, 2018

As I learned to float down the river, I found myself feeling more alive. I was paying attention to that inner wisdom, and as I did, the life Rob was leading me into continued to reveal itself.

I was truly learning a whole new way to live, with more freedom and joy.

From: **Dave Stradling**
To: Rob Bell
Date: September 11, 2018

Hey Rob,

I've been practicing this new way of living for a few months now, and I'm feeling more inspired and rested!

I took a bunch of time off at the end of last month and spoke for the first time in a few weeks this Sunday. It felt great! I noticed that over these past few months my sermons have become more simple. It's as if I am finally learning to not cram everything in but I'm giving the ideas space to breathe. In the past I would force an idea, but I'm learning that way of doing things just leaves me stressed and exhausted.

I'm telling more stories because I'm seeing more as I go through my day. This past sermon was a riff on one sentence my acupuncturist said to me the first session I had with him! I'm having more fun too, which I haven't had in a long time. I actually feel like I can do this more long term now, whereas before I was wondering if I could keep up with the pressure I put on myself.

As I re-enter my pastor/speaker life, I see that I'm still learning how to trust myself and what my next step is. I still feel a pull back to the "old way" of needing permission or having to read 50 books on a topic before acting or speaking. I'm sure I just need to continue exercising these new muscles that I'm building—listening to my soul and acting on it, being aware of my energy/inspiration levels, scheduling around seasons and not overloading, keeping space for play, silence—silence is one I haven't done well, but I feel a pull within me for more of it.

Overall I feel different, as if there is something building up within me, but I have no idea what that is. Maybe I'm starting to live from a different place or truly see things for the first time? I'm just going to keep floating down the river and see where it takes me!

Dave

From: **Rob Bell**
  To: Dave Stradling
Date: September 12, 2018

yes!!!
it's a whole new life, isn't it?
you're playing a different game.
you're living from a different place.
keep floating down that river . . .

This email feels so free. There's a different energy behind it. The weariness and exhaustion present in earlier emails is no longer there.

I'm floating down the river:

Giving myself permission.

Paying attention.

Listening.

Trusting.

Practicing healthy, sustainable, life-filling rhythms.

And I'm . . . getting acupuncture?

The first time I walked into the acupuncturist's office in June 2018, I was nervous. I was going to lie on a table and someone was going to stick needles into me? How could this be a good idea?

But I was determined to reclaim my health, and if my doctor suggested acupuncture, I was willing to give it a try.

As soon as I stepped into the office of Aaron Kwan, my anxiety began to dissipate. His calming presence brought a sense of relief. I immediately knew he was someone who cared for me and my health.

For my first treatment, Aaron flicked eleven needles into my skin with his index finger. I didn't need to be an expert to see that some needles glided in more easily than others. Before leaving the room, he explained why. "I can tell your body is very tense. For some reason, it is unable to relax. You're holding everything tightly. While you're here under my care, your job is to understand why this is. I believe all my patients come here for a reason and this is your reason—to learn to loosen the grip."

Had he been reading my emails? How could he have had all that insight from sticking a few needles into my skin? Here was another invitation to let go and float.

I deeply appreciated the space Aaron created for me. I'd look forward to thirty minutes by myself in the dark with nowhere to go and nothing to do. I could simply be. All my worries and concerns could slip away. Twice a week I'd lie on an exam table with eleven needles, sometimes more, sticking out of my skin.

Each time Aaron would turn off the light, open the door to leave, and say, "Rest now, stressed-out pastor."

Some days I'd fall asleep, only waking as Aaron opened the door to let me know my time was up. It was exactly what I needed.

Aaron's first assessment acknowledged I would be under his care for only a season. Eventually, the season would end. But while I was there, he was offering me a gift. The space to heal. To look deeper into my inner workings.

I knew this was the same gift I wanted to offer those I spoke to each Sunday morning. I told them as much. For however long our paths crossed, I wanted to create a space for everyone to experience the Spirit in the exact place they found themselves. Some needed to heal. Some needed a community of others to walk with them in life. Others needed a new perspective on God, or a place to begin their journey of following Jesus. No matter how long their season lasted, I wanted everyone to receive that same gift Aaron had offered me.

According to my basic understanding, acupuncture works by releasing blocked energy. When the needles are inserted, they release that energy so it can freely flow, triggering the body's natural healing response.

I have no proof that acupuncture "worked." I do know I began to have more energy. I know I began releasing the tight grip I was holding on everything. Things started flowing more smoothly. This email is proof of that.

Through acupuncture, I saw to a greater degree how connected our human elements are. We can't be separated into different parts like body, brain, spirit. It's all one. It's all connected. The tightness, or resistance to needles, was the visible, physical manifestation of was happening in my head. It wasn't confined to one part. It affected the whole.

Some days, the needles would glide right in. Other days they met more resistance. It was a good indicator of how much stress I was carrying or how much pressure I was placing on myself.

By the time I ended my sessions, a year and half later, the needles were easily gliding in more often than not. That tight grip was loosening. The blocked energy was flowing and I kept floating down that river.

Eighteen Questions

Monday, April 22, 2019

In 2014, after Rob offered feedback on my sermon, he asked his first question of me: "What do you think?"

My response was, "I wish I could go back and preach that one again!"

"Why can't you?" he asked.

"I can do that?"

"Why not? Tell everyone you didn't capture the depth of the passage the first time, so you want to show them what you've seen since then."

At the time, I couldn't contemplate admitting my sermon was lacking. I'd put so much time, study, and effort into it. Admitting I didn't get it "right" would be a sign of defeat. It was another warped idea of what I thought people expected of me. It was a rigid view. Inflexible, with little space for continued growth. I was supposed to be the expert and couldn't admit otherwise. People were looking to me for the answers, and I had to provide them.

Rob was trying to show me that it's OK to admit being in process. I didn't have to have it all figured out. In fact, there's no way I could ever have it all figured out. Like everyone else, I was on a never-ending journey of discovery. Acknowledging that truth would not only remove my anxiety, it would offer others the permission to be OK with their personal and unique journey.

I carried that weight with me for a long time. It was one of the many pressures that hovered over me as I tried forcing my path forward instead of allowing myself grace to walk it one step at a time. It was my 2018 sermon series on Colossians that brought awareness to this exhausting belief.

Fresh off my period of burnout, I found myself being pulled right back to where I'd been before. The excitement I initially felt from returning quickly transformed into an overwhelming pressure. I was reading so many new ideas. I couldn't accumulate knowledge fast enough. My reading stack was growing by the day, while I was becoming less confident in my ability to write sermons that conveyed the vastness of what the letter to the Colossians was saying.

But this time, the pressure didn't fully overtake me. In the middle of the series, I came to the realization that no one was stopping me from preaching more sermons on this ancient letter sometime in the future. I laugh now. This truth sounds so simple and basic. How had I missed it? At the time, it was life altering. Immediately, I felt a weight lift. I didn't have to know everything. Wherever I was on my journey was OK. There was no pressure to be anywhere other than where I was. That was enough. I could give these sermons, trusting

I'll continue journeying deeper into the truths I was just beginning to discover. And that would birth a whole host of other sermons without the back-breaking effort.

The damaging expectations shaping me also created a set of rules to live by. They defined what was and wasn't allowed. Preaching on a passage twice was apparently on the "not allowed" list. Many of my emails show me wrestling with these rules. Deep down, I know it's me establishing the rules, but I'm unable to fully act on that truth. I have one foot in freedom and one in a self-imposed prison.

From: **Dave Stradling**
To: Rob Bell
Date: April 22, 2019

Hi Rob!

I'm still going and watching my notebook fill up! I've noticed how things appear to move slower. This doesn't happen all the time and sometimes I fall out of this practice, but overall it feels like I'm experiencing things at a deeper level because I am taking the time to record and reflect on what I'm experiencing (even if at the time I'm not sure what it's doing within me). It's like I'm now starting to see the hidden truths all around me. It also seems to be making me more mindful and less reactionary. The only way I can describe it is as if I'm finding more space.

I'm also seeing and actually believing for the first time that I'm on a journey. So much of my anxiety was created by me thinking that the sermon I was giving had to be the definitive word on the passage/topic/etc. Now I'm seeing that I could preach the same passage or topic every year, and I would come at it from a different perspective because I'm growing and being exposed to different things which are shaping me. I guess that's the flow—trusting the river is leading me to new and different places all the time. My only job is to be aware of what's around me.

It really is a different place to live from, and I get frustrated that so few people seem to even want this way of living. How do you stay inspired and resilient when you're trying to show others this way of living and they're still sitting on the couch? Is it selfish to want this way of living simply for me and hope that it will help people as I keep going?

And should I be trying to organize the notebook in any way? I have stories/ideas/observations and lots of book notes and quotes but no real way of organizing everything. Should I spend the time trying to arrange things somewhere so I can access them later, or should I be flipping through my notebook from time to time to see what's there? I now have material but don't always know what to do with it.

Thanks!

Dave

From: **Rob Bell**
To: Dave Stradling
Date: April 25, 2019

dave, what a great email—i'm so happy to hear all that
you're learning and experiencing. it is like a river! haha
now, onto your questions which bring me to some questions:
you mention it's frustrating for you when people don't
seem to want what you're talking about.
did you?
earlier—did you want this?
because this is new for you, correct?
so what was it that opened you up?
what made you interested in a different way of living?
go back through your story,
did people being frustrated with you ever help you?
when someone was frustrated with you,
did that make you want what they had?

what was it that cracked you open in new ways?
what was it about certain people that made you curious?

next questions . . .
you used the word SHOULD a few times.
do you see what you did there?
what does "should" imply?
i've been watching you trust your deepest self more and
more and more and more

you're learning to listen for the truth that you already
possess, what you already know . . .
SHOULD implies . . . what?
that there are rules?
that you're doing it right or wrong?
you left that behind, didn't you?
that haunting sense that there's one way and you
need to find it . . .
the better question:
what's working for you?
what's opening you up?
what's inspiring you?

From: **Dave Stradling**
  To: Rob Bell
Date: April 25, 2019

So you're saying I haven't arrived? Haha.

I get it, I'm still assuming there's one way to do it. I'm still trying to force the river along instead of observing what I'm experiencing. But the path is to go deeper in. Instead of looking externally, I need to keep looking inside for where I'm finding life and trust that.

And yes, getting frustrated won't help me or anyone. The only thing that helped me was observing people whose presence made me want what they had. They didn't seem to care about the results; they were being true to what they were learning/experiencing and then bearing witness to that reality, which is way more compelling for others and freeing for me. That's what I wanted; to see people free in themselves.

The path of unlearning and relearning continues!

From: **Rob Bell**

To: Dave Stradling

Date: April 26, 2019

yes! it's even more fun than you thought . . .

Eighteen questions. Every one hitting the nail on the head.

Learning to shake my belief in some master playbook has not been easy. Life has always seemed to exist as a series of rules to follow. There's a right way to do things, and a wrong way. I've spent much energy and mental space trying to discover that elusive right way.

This started at a young age. One Saturday night in elementary school, I went to a friend's house. We were flipping through the TV channels when we came across *Mrs. Doubtfire*. My friend and his whole family wanted to watch the movie, but I wasn't thirteen yet and I knew it was rated PG-13, so I told them I couldn't watch it. Yeah, we're talking that level of rule-following. That story still makes us both laugh.

I guess I believed following the rules would keep me safe. As long as you're following the rules, you can't get hurt. You can't fail. You'll be successful and get where you're supposed to go.

I see it so clearly now. I was afraid of failing. This was why I'd created the expectations. It's why I was living by certain rules. It's what caused me to seek others' permission before stepping out. I desperately wanted to be successful and I thought I could find my way there through hard work and always getting it right. I was going to prove I belonged.

It took me long enough, but I finally see what was keeping me stuck: my definition of success.

Like so many other areas of my life, I was looking outside myself for this definition. It was another external pursuit. I was looking at all the ways I didn't measure up to the ideas of success that had been created for me.

My idea of a successful church and what would validate me as a pastor and a person were wrapped up in many of the churches I initially looked to for inspiration. They were large congregations, easily attracting hundreds of people each week. This was not what Awaken looked like. We were declining in church attendance when I wrote this email. Moving in the opposite direction of my idea of success. In fact, our leadership team was wondering how much longer we as a church could be sustainable.

It resurrected all the old questions of frustration.

Why aren't people getting it?

Why aren't we growing?

Why don't more people want to walk this path I'm leading them down?

Yes, the frustrations were externally focused. But they were exposing an inner tension. I've found this is often the case. Our harsh critique of others typically finds its source in an unresolved piece of our own lives. Look within and you'll discover where the true frustration lies.

Before starting a church, I sought out the advice of others who had walked that road before me. One piece of advice came in the form of a question.

"Are you starting this church for yourself or for others?"

It took some time to answer because I'd been trained to believe starting a church was only for others. It was a selfless act. But as I thought about how to answer, I realized it was also for me.

Yes, I wanted to create a space for others to experience God. But I also wanted to start a church that was true to the journey I was on. I wanted freedom to explore my path. From the beginning I knew I couldn't fully pursue both without launching off on my own.

Years later, I had forgotten the "for me" part.

I was so focused on the externals, I was missing the joy of my journey.

Growing a large church is what success looked like in the world I was swimming in. It was one of the first questions pastors asked each other: "How large is your church?" As if we were sizing each other up to see who was more successful. Being in that environment, always being the one with the smallest congregation, wore me down by feeding my insecurities and creating frustration. It made me constantly question if I was doing the right thing. Wondering why I wasn't as successful as others.

Rob's eighteen questions in his latest email refocused my attention inward. They pointed me back to why I started Awaken in the first place. As I wrestled with these questions over the next few months, I came to realize I didn't have to be confined to others' definition of success.

I was free to create my own definition. A definition true to the person I was. This was the spark I'd lost from my younger years, when I wasn't looking to others for approval, but finding joy in walking the path opening before me. It was this life I wanted for myself.

No longer did I need to play the comparison game.

If I would just keep following my path,

looking within,

finding joy in that pursuit,

I would discover the success I truly desired.

A type of success that produced life within me instead of frustration from seeking out something that wasn't mine.

The Gift of Reframing

For years I was the loyal soldier, dutifully doing what I was supposed to do. I'd turned everything into a chore. My role as pastor. My personal faith. It was all about my effort. My ability to discern the true path. There was no room for the Spirit. I was trying to do it all on my own. Shouldering the full weight of this path to Jesus by taking responsibility for every cause and pushing myself to get everyone to follow this path I was trying so hard to walk.

I was only letting the river carry me so much. My oars were still in the water while I hoped I could speed things along and direct the flow. And I was trying to pack everyone into the boat with me. I wasn't entrusting anyone else's path to the flow of the river—the leading of the Spirit in their life.

Of course such a life would feel heavy.

I was trying to save the world but didn't know where to start.

From: **Dave Stradling**

To: Rob Bell

Date: July 1, 2019

Hey Rob!

I'm working on the "no rules" part of my work. I polled our group for questions and topics they wanted to discuss and now follow up each sermon with a live Q&A. It's been a blast and people are loving it. I'm seeing it's a different skill I'm having to develop and am enjoying the journey of needing to be even more calm and centered up there.

One topic that was suggested was "political groups and God." I took a first stab at it yesterday which went well. Let's just say there was no end to the questions and I couldn't even address all of them, so I'm going to have to follow that one up soon. I was wondering if you have any books you could recommend on that topic so I can develop my thinking a bit more. This is an area I haven't thought too much about, but judging from yesterday, a lot of people want to talk about it. I've listened to your Robcast episodes on it from a few years back which were helpful!

Thanks!

Dave

From: **Rob Bell**
  To: Dave Stradling
Date: July 2, 2019

oh man, i'm so happy to hear this, dave.

i can feel the lightness and joy in your email.

two books to start with:

first

john dominic crossan's jesus: a revolutionary biography

and then walsh and keesmaat have a book on colossians

called remixed

amazing

start there

tell me what you think

From: **Dave Stradling**
  To: Rob Bell
Date: September 18, 2019

Hey Rob!

I finished reading *Colossians Remixed* and Crossan's *Jesus* and am feeling both inspired and disturbed at the same time. I definitely have enough material for the next year of sermons!

Colossians Remixed with its modern reading is especially disturbing. Reading what they wrote made me see how entwined Christianity and my life are with the very way of living that Jesus and Paul in Colossians were combating. It's even overwhelming! Where do I start? How can I critique a way of life that I myself am complicit in? I could easily (and I'm sure many people do) write off what they're saying as extreme, but I see the truth in their words. Ha, it would have been easier to never have read the book. Now I have to wrestle with what it means for my life.

It challenges my comfort and the systems I've created for my life. Money in the stock market, supporting corporations, etc. Do I really have to give up Star Wars! I appreciate their emphasis on patience. I read this and immediately want to change everything, but I know it doesn't work that way. This happens over time and with many more conversations and thought. But who is having these conversations? They're clearly absent in the church. How do I keep learning and growing outside of books?

It makes me want to keep going down the path I'm on and keep pushing it further. Which at the same time is intimidating because it will require more of me. And I'm sure more sacrifice. Does my resistance mean I'm not ready yet? I do feel like I'm being led down this path, I just don't fully know what it will look like. I know I'm not living all of this now. How do I live and support my family while immersed in this system?

One thing that stood out was that wrestling with this requires space and time. Something that we rarely have today. Which is why these ideas never get addressed—we look for the convenient and easy. The whole idea of me living a different way so I can lead others down that path is so necessary. The anxiety and busyness of modern society seems to be crippling even the possibility of this type of life.

And then what about helping people now? I see how you could get so caught up in these large, important issues but also neglect helping people live their lives in the day to day, which I'm realizing most people are having a hard-enough time doing.

Those are some initial thoughts after reading!

Dave

This first response of mine shows how the books challenged me. They were painting a way of following Jesus that was inspiring me. However, rather than seeing an adventure ahead, I saw a burden to carry. All these new ideas became new rules to live by. More things I had to do. What's more, this was my second read-through of *Colossians Remixed*. I'd read it a few years earlier during my Colossians sermon series and all the ideas I hadn't acted on became a reminder of what I wasn't doing. Why hadn't I made these changes yet?!

I was imagining an ideal way of living. This ideal was constantly changing based on what I was learning. I saw my inability to reach that ever-changing ideal as a flaw in who I was. What was wrong with me that I couldn't be more than who I was at that moment? Why couldn't I do more? I was overly critical of myself, which resurrected old feelings of frustration and reactivity.

I was once again experiencing "imposter syndrome." Doubting myself. Questioning if I was ready. Wondering if I had what it took to embody this life I was reading about. It left me paralyzed—unable to take a step in the direction I was being led. I was looking at the whole. Thinking I had to change everything at once instead of breaking the whole into parts and acting on one idea at a time. I felt powerless to even begin.

I can feel the anxiety pouring out of this email—it's no wonder those acupuncture needles often had a difficult time working their way in!

Rob's response was enlightening.

From: **Rob Bell**
To: Dave Stradling
Date: September 19, 2019

oh man, dave, this is getting exciting, isn't it?
a few comments below

> Where do I start?

awareness is the start
you see things you didn't see before
what a gift!
instead of shame, how about gratitude?
this is how things change: we see what we didn't see before
and then gradually our lives get adjusted around what we see

> How can I critique a way of life that I myself am complicit in?

jesus talked about the kingdom being like a seed that
gets planted.
and seeds take time.
they grow.
gradually.
see the weight that takes off?

trust the truth, dave.
it's very, very powerful.
you've had your eyes opened,
and you're going to subtly be responding to these
new truths in all sorts of ways.
you don't have to do anything overnight
be careful not to swap one fundamentalism for another.
this is why people who get fired up about these issues can be
so abrasive and ultimately end up turning people off.
they get too in your face
too harsh

start with yourself
follow it where it leads
see what you learn
make a change here
change a habit there
the spirit will tell you
relax
you'll know what to do
one step at a time

see what sticks
what doesn't

when i stumbled into all this,
kristen and i decided to buy a former crack house
and move into the city
it was dangerous
and new and exciting
it was a big radical change in response to what we
were learning
i loved it
at first
but there was so much work to be done in the neighborhood
that began to take up my time
and i had less and less energy to do the work i'm here to do
see what i mean?
we jumped in
we learned
we had experiences
we made changes in response to those

GIVE YOURSELF GRACE
grace
grace
grace
you're open
you're learning
try something

see what it leads to
drop it if it's too heavy
grace grace grace

> Ha, it would have been easier to never have read
> the book. Now I have to wrestle with what it means
> for my life.

how about changing your language here?
because how we name things shapes what happens.
how about instead of
have to
you change it to
get to?
instead of wrestling or a trial or struggle, how about an invitation?
or an adventure?
see how much better that naming is?
how it liberates and empowers and invigorates?

> Do I really have to give up Star Wars!

no, you don't
good God, man,
star wars stays
life is about joy

> But who is having these conversations? They're
> clearly absent in the church.

oh man, these conversations are happening all over the place
and tons of them are happening in churches

there are churches right now that can talk about nothing else
be careful not to universalize your particular experience
there are lots of traditions that have these conversations
at the center of all they do
have you read walter brueggemann?
that guy goes around the world stoking these conversations
and thousands of people are participating

> It makes me want to keep going down the path I'm
> on and keep pushing it further.

how about changing from
pushing
to
following?
see the shift there
pushing can get exhausting
but following
that's about curiosity

> Which at the same time is intimidating because it
> will require more of me.

remember that in hebrews we read that jesus
goes to the cross
for the joy set before him.
boom!
see that?
joy.
you get to explore new ways of living that are better

for you and the world.
let it be that.

i just bought an electric car.
we're about to put solar panels on our house.
we'll be off the electric here in no time.
so much fun.
we just gave so much stuff away to people who need it.
that was more fun than buying anything . . .

see what i mean?
follow it,
and you'll never stop finding wonderful ways to serve
and give and live more simply.

> How do I still live and support my family while
> immersed in this system?

here's the thing about systems:
you have to live in them to a certain extent.
paul, who wrote those letters, traveled, right?
on what roads?
roman roads!
the very system he's resisting built roads to
more easily conquer—
and he used those roads to travel around spreading resistance.
get it?
you need food, clothes, a roof over your head—
everybody is participating at some level.

you can't be totally free,

paul wasn't.

but you can resist.

and take steps.

and be dangerous.

and have fun.

you can do that.

that's the jesus invitation . . .

to be in it but not of it—

that passage starts to make more sense, doesn't it?

> One thing that stood out was that wrestling with this requires space and time. Something that we rarely have today.

why not?

why do you not have space and time?

what are you doing that's more important than that?

i am pushing you here and i love it!

stay with me—

why not?

what if that's your first step?

make space and time.

honor it. respect it.

in some ways, it's your job!

so do it.

slow down. reflect. get rid of what doesn't matter.

say no more.

| Which is why these ideas never get addressed

they get addressed all the time.
check out carl honoré's work—
there's an explosion of new literature and sites dedicated
to simplicity and fair trade and better business practices.

> The whole idea of me living a different way so I
> can lead others down that path is so necessary.
> The anxiety and busyness of modern society
> seems to be crippling even the possibility of this
> type of life.

is this your calling?
is this why this has you so worked up?
because you're realizing that you can't change a system until
you've taken steps yourself?
so take a step.
say a prayer, ask for one thing
one step you can take today
take it
enjoy taking it
see what happens

> And then what about helping people now? I see
> how you could get so caught up in these large,
> important issues but also neglect helping people
> live their lives in the day to day which I'm realizing
> most people are having a hard-enough time doing.

dude, you get it.
slow it all down.

give yourself to living a meaningful, sustainable life.
sort out your life.
and watch.
you'll effortlessly see that you're helping people all over
the place without even trying.
that's how it works.
it's about to get really fun, dave.

From: **Dave Stradling**
  To: Rob Bell
Date: September 19, 2019

Reading your comments made my heart pump a little faster!

I can feel the excitement of the adventure.

Yes, it's all new, and I don't know what will happen, where it will go, what will stick, or what will stay.

Thanks for calling out my "work/striving/have to/performance" mentality.

You're right, joy wasn't the first thing I thought of, but that's the only way anything will be sustainable, the only way I will continue following this path, and the only way I will invite others into this journey.

I feel like I've been really good at following my curiosity through reading, but not as good as taking action on it, almost as if I'm thinking, could I ever really do this, or what if I'm wrong or take a misstep?

But seeds and grace and discerning the heaviness or lightness ... YES!

That's the exciting part.

That's an invitation rather than a burden.

Your observation about what I'm called to do, and what my work is, I think I'm still learning that part.

I catch glimpses of moments when I feel alive but feel there's more for me to explore here. I will need to keep cutting things and saying no.

There is absolutely no reason why I can't create an anxiety-less, joyful, simpler way of life where I am.

I am definitely not doing anything more important than that!

I often look at the church I started and get upset because it's not growing fast enough or I'm not in front of enough people, but that's just taking me further away from this type of life.

Maybe that restlessness is really a restlessness within my own soul for not relentlessly pursuing my life and the steps that are already in front of me.

I even thought about applying for another church job, but I know that will not be the thing that brings me joy.

What a fun path—exploring things and then reporting back to others what I've discovered along the way.

That's what I want to do.

That's where I have found the life.

I need to stop trying to control everything and everyone and just live!

And definitely watch more Star Wars.

Thank you!

From: **Rob Bell**
  To: Dave Stradling
Date: September 19, 2019

yes to all of it—
do you see the leaps of insight you're making here?
really profound.
and do you see how warped views of the cross have
shaped life for so many?
what those warped views do is give people the
idea that it has to be hard. that they have to suffer.
and so they take grace and adventure and invitation and
turn it into another way to suffer because, well, jesus did.
but that isn't the point, is it?
for the joy.

and you are so right about your own life.
start making whatever small changes announce
themselves to you that you can do right now,

not with guilt or strain but with lightness and hope.
start there.
and don't preach at anybody.
just follow your path.
and then tell people about the love you're experiencing.
that's how it works!

From: **Dave Stradling**
  To: Rob Bell
Date: September 20, 2019

So the suffering is never sought out, it might just happen because of the path I'm on or simply because difficult moments arise.

The real path is pursuing what makes me come alive, and then the suffering becomes joy as Paul talks about and Jesus experienced.

Any of the guilt I feel about not busting it enough is all self-induced because I'm after something different so I can help others see something different.

And I can't carry every burden myself. I can show people what I'm learning and what I'm experiencing, but I can't expect to throw myself into every single area in the world that needs help and healing.

I guess that's been tripping me up. I've been paralyzed because I put this pressure on myself to do it all and be everything, but that's not my path.

Haha, you know, I think I've been operating from the mindset that my path is TOO GOOD TO BE TRUE.

It's been heavy because I've been carrying too much responsibility and trying to walk too many paths.

Too much weight and not enough grace or adventure or joy.

This is really helpful.

A much-needed change in perspective and framing language in order to create a new world to swim in!

———

From: **Rob Bell**
  To: Dave Stradling
Date: September 20, 2019

yes yes yes
you see how life-changing this is!
and you are so right.
if it seems too good to be true,
that's called grace
go in that direction

One of the gifts Rob has given me is the gift of reframing. I'd often be stuck or overwhelmed because of how I looked at a situation. By changing the language I was using and asking different questions, my perspective shifted. The limited, paralyzing story I was telling expanded. Opportunities that were once hidden emerged as I discovered the joy that had been present the entire time.

This is what happened here.

To begin with, I was looking at all these new ways of living as a duty or obligation. I even lamented the fact I'd been exposed to these ideas. I thought life would be better if I kept my head in the sand, closing myself off to anything that challenged me and my beliefs. I wanted to go back to an easier time when things were black and white. A time when someone else gave me the answers. Told me what to do and what to believe. But, as I'd been seeing, there was no going back. I had witnessed too much.

My first response and the two subsequent ones read as if two different people wrote them. There's the first one: my initial thoughts on the two books. Then, there's my follow-up to Rob's comments. In between, something within me shifted.

I was facing a choice. I could create excuses for why these new ways of living were impossible. This is exactly what's happening in the first half of this email exchange. I'm retreating. Shrinking back in on myself. This is a totally normal response when we feel challenged. But I'd come too far to turn my back on what I was seeing. That would only lead to endless frustration for not having the courage to take another step forward.

Or, I could look at all I was learning as a gift.

An opportunity.

An adventure.

An invitation into a better way of living, more true to the person I was.

When Rob reframed it in that way, lights immediately started turning on. There's an energy and enthusiasm in my response that was absent earlier. I was making connections with all I'd been discovering through my previous emails. All the seemingly independent truths I'd found scattered along the trail were coming together to form a cohesive whole.

By the end of this email exchange, I realized I'd still been allowing external voices to shape the stories guiding my life. But now I saw that I had the power to choose the story. I didn't have to place others' stories on myself. Just like my definition of success, I could allow the narrative I lived by to be shaped from within.

At that moment, I chose to see the path ahead of me as a gift. I flipped the obligatory tone of "I have to walk this path" to "I get to walk this path."

And there's a huge difference between feeling you have to walk a certain path and choosing to walk a path. Each approach creates a world wholly different from the other. I could choose which of those worlds my steps would create.

There's a Scripture passage I often use as I serve Eucharist. It's a saying of Jesus found in the Gospel of Matthew.

"Come to me, all you who are weary and burdened, and I will give you rest. Take my yoke upon you and learn from me, for I am gentle and humble in heart, and you will find rest for your souls. For my yoke is easy and my burden is light."[4]

My burden is light.

This life of lightness and joy and grace is what I would invite others into each week, but I wasn't experiencing it myself.

---

4   Matthew 11:28-30 NIV

When I felt weary or burdened, I rarely stopped to rest. I didn't pause to explore why I felt that way. I kept going. It was my responsibility to sacrifice for the people. And if I could just sacrifice a little more, the church would grow.

I'd been closing myself off to the grace I invited others into. I couldn't believe my path as pastor was something I could enjoy. I'm not sure I believed faith was something to enjoy. If there wasn't a struggle, I must not be taking my faith or role as pastor seriously enough.

As I opened myself up to the grace in front of me, I began experiencing the easy yoke and light burden Jesus spoke about. The heavy weight of responsibility started lifting. I could seek out simplicity and forgo the cult of continuously piling one activity on top of another. I no longer had to support every cause. I didn't have to say yes to every invitation I received. It was even OK to try carrying something and drop it after a few steps if it was too heavy. I could cheer others on without having to be intimately involved in everything.

This freed me to say yes to my path. I was free to experiment. See what worked for me. What was leading me deeper into life. I didn't have to deny myself this grace any longer. I could embrace the joy, trusting as I did that I would be living a life true to the person I was and would effortlessly discover all I had been working so hard to achieve.

Coronavirus

Wednesday, March 18, 2020

The first week we canceled our in-person services due to the pandemic, I placed enormous pressure on myself to give the perfect sermon. Not giving the sermon live allowed me to record as many takes as necessary to get every detail how I wanted it. I must have tried at least six times before I gave up, each time stopping the recording when I didn't feel it was good enough. Editing the video wasn't an option because we didn't have a production team. I knew enough to hit Record and upload the file to YouTube. That was it.

After chasing the perfect recording for a full day, I gave up and did it live at my kitchen table the following morning. Our kids were playing in the other room. It was perfect. Low key, laid back, authentic.

Then came the realization I would have to do it again. COVID-19 wasn't going to be resolved in a week.

At the start of the pandemic, I got stuck in my head. I started overthinking instead of feeling my way through the uncertainty.

There was no trust or flow. I was back in control mode. Even my body reverted to the familiar way of holding itself tightly. The morning after attempting to record the perfect sermon, I woke up with a stiff neck, barely able to turn it left or right.

This way of living, I knew, would not lead to the calming, non-anxious presence I desired.

From: **Dave Stradling**
To: Rob Bell
Date: March 18, 2020

Hey Rob,

Thanks for your two podcasts on the coronavirus—it's really helped me process what's going on and gave me the permission to be OK with how I'm feeling.

Something felt off in me seeing every church's sermon this weekend being "faith/courage over fear" and you helped me recognize why I was feeling that way—numbing the feelings instead of entering into what's happening.

My wife has severe asthma and we have a five-month-old, so I'm obviously a bit more on edge, considering we're a hotspot right outside NYC.

I know people are looking to me for some guidance and stability, and I'm feeling the pressure.

I've had to help more at home with two young kids and no childcare so that's limiting my "work time."

I know that's my main responsibility right now but also want to help our church make sense of it all.

I'm trying to feel my way through it—I video-recorded my sermon last week at the breakfast table, really laid back, and this week I have a bunch of thoughts written down about what I'm experiencing.

Is that my role right now? To process publicly what I am experiencing? It doesn't feel right to go back to the series I was in amid such massive upheaval.

I know I'm to be as calm and non-anxious as possible so I can be that presence for people. I just don't want sermon prep to become a stressor.

Haha, there was no class in seminary about this! I am learning as I go. Any suggestions you can offer me as I continue navigating this?

Thank you!

Dave

———————————

From: **Rob Bell**
  To: Dave Stradling
Date: March 19, 2020

seriously, dave, you know exactly what to do.
do you see how much wisdom there is in that email you sent me?
go back through and read it.
do you see what you're leaving behind?

the idea that there's some truth or wisdom or insight or plan
that is outside of you and you need to do something
to go get it.

see that?
you're leaving that whole dis-ease behind.
because you know what to do.
see that part about doing the sermon from your table?
that's brilliant.
and so helpful
and now you have some thoughts about how you're feeling?
great.
don't overthink it
hit record and tell your people those thoughts
give them that gift
they don't need a polished orator
we all need to be together
presence

got it?

while we're at it—let's get rid of that phrase "work time"
it doesn't work, does it?
i know.
your life is a gift, dave.
let the whole thing be a gift.
pay attention to all of it.
be present to your family like never before.

notice it all.
share with your church what you're seeing.

do you feel how clean and elegant that feels?
no need to gunk it up
especially with a new series on something distracting.

now, let's take it farther, shall we?
you mentioned other churches talking about fear etc
why don't you talk about that?
go all the way into the heart of it?
the temptation to numb
and to use religion to numb the very real feelings
show your people that isn't the tradition
the tradition is to feel it all
and to trust the divine is in all of it

see how there's a powerful sermon right in what you
emailed me?
tell them what you told me

you know exactly what to do.
and then next week, trust that you'll know what to do.
and then the next week . . .
let this whole thing be an invitation for you to open
your heart up
and lead these precious people like never before.
sound good?

From: **Dave Stradling**
To: Rob Bell
Date: March 19, 2020

That sounds great!

After I emailed you, I had this feeling that I already know what to do! I had a bit of a panic moment and forgot that for a minute.

Almost as if I needed permission and was slipping back to my old way of following certain "rules."

I just finished collecting my thoughts and now I'm ready to hit the record button tomorrow morning and let it rip.

Yes, I'm using exactly what I emailed you—that is the gift. Unpacking what I'm experiencing to help others sort through what they're experiencing.

It's as if I'm giving them the same permission that I was looking for—the permission to enter in and feel it all.

That definitely takes the pressure off, and I'm excited to unleash this one and whatever else I will stumble upon in the coming weeks.

It feels like a joy again, which feels odd to say in the current disruption.

Thank you!

When I hit Record the following day, I was sitting at my patio table. I hadn't written a manuscript. Instead, I had a small stack of index cards with words and phrases on them. Those were my notes. It was my first time ever preaching without a manuscript. And it felt great. I wasn't trying to memorize anything. I was simply witnessing to all I was seeing and it flowed out of me.

After releasing the sermon, I received emails and texts from people, some I hadn't heard from in a while, telling me how helpful the sermon was. It connected with people. It helped give others permission to be OK with wherever they were with their own fears, concerns, and anxieties about this new, uncertain moment in history.

Then, the next week, I did it again. Just me at that same patio table with more index cards.

That's how it went for those first few weeks of the COVID pandemic. I'd keep my notebook close by so I could capture the stories, feelings, and thoughts that were helping me make sense of it all. When it was time to record my weekly sermon, I'd go to the patio, open my notebook, and talk about everything I was observing. Never once did I struggle with finding something to say. There was always plenty of material in my notebook.

Now, let's rewind to my panic moment before I slid into that routine.

2020 was supposed to be a big year for Awaken. It was the year we were hoping to get our attendance numbers back up. Questions about sustainability had been hovering over the church for a few years. That hope quickly faded when COVID struck and our services moved online for the foreseeable future. We weren't equipped to be an online church, but that's what we became.

Before recording that first online sermon, I'd seen some well-produced digital services released by other churches. I felt intimidated, wondering how we would ever compete. They had the camera, the lights, and a nice stage. We had none of that. All I had was a laptop. Yes, a laptop. A techie friend watched some of those early sermons and said, "It looks like you're using your laptop." When I told him I was, he laughed. Then he helped us research cameras.

I was once again trying to control outcomes, taking on the weight of responsibilities that weren't mine to carry. It started to feel like a burden. I was neglecting to see the gift of the moment. That I get to give a sermon.

So I didn't have the best technology. I could still give a sermon. I could still talk to others about what I was seeing. What I was feeling. Where I was experiencing the divine presence. That was my unique gift to offer.

I was feeling weighed down because I believed I had to give something that wasn't mine to give. Yes, I wouldn't be able to rival the production quality of other churches. It didn't matter. That was out of my control. What I could control was how present I was to life. That was where the sermons would be birthed from.

And, as Rob reminded me, I was already doing this. He showed me the inner wisdom I already possessed. I didn't need to seek anything out. It was all right there. He was giving me permission to be me.

I ran with that permission.

Thirty-Seven Minutes

Thursday, May 7, 2020

I based my next sermon on the last email I sent Rob. How light it felt. How easily it flowed. Sitting on my back patio with my kids staring out at me through a window felt genuine. I wasn't trying to be more than who I was. I let go of all outcomes, including the future of the church. I spent more time outdoors. Enjoyed the extra time at home with our new family of four. I found myself being filled with life.

As the weeks went by, I gained more confidence. When I recorded my sermons, instead of a manuscript, I had a one- or two-page handwritten outline. I was trusting that, in the moment, the details would emerge. This was a truth Rob had passed along years earlier which I was now discovering to be true.

One week I was completely gassed. The ideas weren't coming. My notebook pages were blank, and I was going to use an interview I'd recorded as the sermon for the week. But then I had a feeling to hit Record and just start talking. Thirty-seven minutes later, I had my sermon. I couldn't believe it.

Of course, I had to give Rob an update on all I was experiencing.

From: **Dave Stradling**
To: Rob Bell
Date: May 7, 2020

Rob!

These past few weeks have been pretty amazing. It's as if my sermons have gone to a different level. I've been keeping a notebook full of ideas and things I'm noticing and then each week I record those observations. It's been amazing. The feedback has been great. It's as if I'm freer than I've ever been before.

Last week I was stuck. We're talking really stuck. I couldn't formulate an outline and I almost threw in the towel on recording a sermon and used an interview I had already recorded. But I had this sense to just hit Record and do it. So I did, and I started talking about being stuck and that led from one idea to the next. When I hit Stop, I looked down and saw I had spoken for thirty-seven minutes! It was unreal how it all just flowed together. I was surprising myself with what was popping into my mind and where the sermon was going. It really was the first time I completely got out of my head. It felt so different, but so full of life!

Through all of it, I feel I'm becoming different. I'm way more confident in my message and myself. I received some criticism of a sermon, but rather than backtrack, I held my ground and graciously tried showing how I saw things differently. I'm actually allowing myself freedom to go where I want to go with my ideas. It has been great and I feel so much more alive.

Thank you for continuing to open my eyes to the flow and encouraging me to trust that inner wisdom. I'm seeing it and feeling it more and more!

Dave

From: **Rob Bell**
  To: Dave Stradling
Date: May 8, 2020

oh man, dave.
what an email!
do you notice how significant it is?
there isn't one
should
or
ought
or
supposed to
in it anywhere.

here's another way to say it:
there isn't any voice on your shoulder.

this is huge.
i'm so happy for you.
freedom, different, alive, flow—
these are the words that bring the life!
so exciting.
i'm cheering you on.
grace and peace,
Rob

This growing confidence continued to change me. It was like an arrow pointing me toward my true path.

The more alive I felt, the more I wanted to keep exploring what I was seeing around me. Ideas started flowing.

As the year continued, I was sensing something building within. The space afforded by a slower pace of life was leading me further into all the truths I'd been learning. Opening my eyes to places where I continued to grip tightly. I became aware of toxic beliefs I was still carrying in my head and how they were closing my heart off to grace and love and life. With each realization, there came a greater sense of freedom. It was as if space was opening inside my heart.

By the end of 2020, there was a new resolve within me. I was ready to jump into 2021 filled with a level of excitement about my work I hadn't experienced before.

More Dave than Ever

Thursday, January 14, 2021

It was in October 2017, during my first meeting with a therapist, when I was first confronted with the idea of shadow-boxing myself. That idea opened my eyes to how I'd been sabotaging my life.

Like most moments of self-awareness, that realization took years for me to fully grasp. I had been made aware of what I was doing but was unaware of how deeply it affected my life. Or even how intertwined this way of being had become with my identity.

As my awareness grew, I began seeing the crippling expectations I was carrying around. In my head was a litany of voices. Every decision was filtered through those voices. It was exhausting. I couldn't walk my path because my true voice was drowned out by other voices.

Finally, I came to a place where I was ready to put the gloves down and step out of the ring.

From: **Dave Stradling**

To: Rob Bell

Date: January 14, 2021

Hey Rob!

I wanted to give you an update on what I'm seeing.

I've been having this overwhelming sense to get even more serious about my work. The words that keep coming to mind are "declutter" and "simplify" in EVERY area of my life. I feel I've been cluttering things up and it's taking me away from exploring and seeing. This is where I am right now. The declutter phase. I have this feeling. I just know this is what I have to do. Simplify all of it and become even more ruthless in saying no and letting go.

The other week I was recording a video sermon since we're not meeting in person. I was cluttering up my content by trying to learn how to use a new higher-quality camera and wanting to overlay pictures on the video but it was all getting in my way. I finally gave all that up, went in my backyard, set up my phone, and hit Record. It was great. Simple and true to me.

In all of this, I realize I've been the one allowing myself to get cluttered. It's as if I have been fighting some imaginary opponent, believing someone or something is preventing me from moving in the direction where I feel the Spirit moving and the topics that I want to explore and talk about. But I see that it's just me. I've been projecting my own inner struggle on others when no one is really forcing me into a box. I'm the one doing it to myself. As if I don't trust myself enough or aren't allowing myself to go wherever this leads me. I'm seeing all of this and am beginning to look at everything and how I've been operating. It's exciting and a bit daunting. What will I discover? Where will this really lead me? What do I possess within? What have I been missing?

Mixed into all of this has been this drive that I have to expand beyond my current role. There's a book I've been working on and I have ideas for other projects I want to pursue. I've been telling myself if I just had more time or didn't have the church to worry about, I could really get some stuff created. But I'm seeing this isn't true. This way of thinking is actually taking me away from my work, thinking the church is in the way of where I "should be."

But what do I do with this desire to get my work in front of more people? How do I pursue it in a way that feels authentic to me as well as not letting that pursuit take over? These are questions I'm exploring. Do I just do the work and see how it lands? Or do I, in some way, actively try to expand my audience? What do you think? Does it sound like I'm trying to push something too hard instead of letting myself be pulled along? Is this another case of me trying too hard and getting in my own way?

Would appreciate any advice on helping me navigate this space.

Thanks!

Dave

From: **Rob Bell**
   To: Dave Stradling
Date: January 15, 2021

Yes—

comments below . . .

> The words that keep coming to mind are "declutter" and "simplify" in EVERY area of my life.

yes, two huge words for me
simplify—i never stop decluttering
and it's a giant wave of fresh air every time
and just when i think i can't get any leaner,
i find another layer to shed, more to say no to
ruthless—we use that word so much in our house
right now, in january, i'm being ruthless in ways
i haven't been before
all because of a deep sense of focus on what this
next chapter is
you're on it!

> The other week I was recording a video sermon since we're not meeting in person. I was cluttering up my content . . . it was all getting in my way.

yep. tech is like that
it can amplify really well and take things to new levels
but it can also get in the way
you can see why so many people become
fundamentalists about this—

they make blanket decisions on what they use, don't use,
instead of simply being present and discerning what to
use at the time
sometimes you go with a nicer camera,
sometimes you use your phone
depends
you'll know from moment to moment
like you did the other week

> In all of this I realize I have been the one allowing
> myself to get cluttered.

one time an older man told me that if it felt heavy
it was because i had picked up something that wasn't
mine to carry
i didn't really get it at the time
but it's so true
so much of this is internal
i'm still learning this
i create this story in my head about what people are needing,
expecting, waiting for
when the real joy is
i'm rob bell and i do it how rob bell does it

which brings us to you
you're right
you get to decide
you get to do it how you do it
this is you properly stepping into your power

because that's the gift you're here to give
if others don't approve or whatever
that is theirs to carry, not yours
your job is to be you
so step into that power
and enjoy it

> Mixed into all of this has been this drive that I have
> to expand beyond my current role.

my first book?
i just wrote it.
i sat at my desk in the middle of the day and wrote it.
know what i mean?
i started making films.
i said yes to speaking offers.
whatever. i just did it.
i did the thing in front of me that i wanted to make,
that i could make.

you get this, don't you, dave?
how i do it now is how i did it then
i knew that the first step was to give myself to giving
great sermons
i knew that there wouldn't be any expansion ever if
the first thing wasn't
done with integrity and passion
i meet people who want to be big
whatever that means

but they aren't giving themselves to the humble work
right in front of them
they'll never get where they want to go like that
you have to humbly serve that which you already have
and then trust that if it's to expand, it will
if you have an idea for a book
don't talk about it
write it
if you have other projects
start on them
don't ask permission

quietly go about following your curiosity
make the things that you want to make
share them with people who you think may enjoy them
let it be whatever it wants to be

so yes, it is totally normal to want to expand
and here's the good news
you can
right now
you don't have to wait for anybody to give you
the green light
you are the green light
have fun

i'm cheering you on
you realize how far you've come from our first emails?

you're more dave than ever

i love it

keep going

What's been interesting to see in these emails is the progression of an idea to an embodied truth. Everything I'm saying here are observations I'd already stumbled upon. But now they're no longer just beliefs I'm holding in my head. Having lived with these beliefs for years and reflected on what they mean for me, I've internalized them. They've become a lens through which I'm understanding my life. What began as awareness has transformed into trust.

Recording that sermon in my backyard provided so much clarity. It was huge for me. In the first week of COVID lockdowns, I'd let those other voices win for a day. It led to complete exhaustion. But this time, I was quicker to notice my energy being drained. Instead of trying to push through, I stopped and focused on that which I could control. I let go of all the pressure and expectation to have mastered a new piece of technology—that could come later. I was trusting what was right for me and ended up creating something I absolutely loved. The sermon was my gift to give. Not a fancy technological production.

I saw it so clearly at that moment. I'd been trying to offer gifts that weren't mine to give. By taking on outside expectations, I was attempting to create or manufacture (a word I used early on in my emails) a gift that was external to me. I was allowing those other voices to define for me what my gift to the world was supposed to be. And then I was working hard to be that person. The years of frustration and exhaustion all made sense. I wasn't being true to me. I finally understood my true gift originates from within. No wonder I felt so empowered after giving this sermon. I was learning to trust the flow, to do it how Dave Stradling does it. I was being true to the person I was. Or, as Rob said, I was stepping into my power.

My emails to Rob show how I've been taking steps in this direction. It was a gradual process. Years in the making. All the questions, struggles, and doubts were me trying to listen for my own voice. To find the life I possessed within instead of a life outside voices were creating for me. Like the sun peeking through the clouds then disappearing again, I had caught glimpses of this life and the freedom it brought, but now the clouds are thinning and the sun is breaking through.

The more freedom I experienced, the more I desired. I wanted to carry less. Travel lighter. Focus my energy on where I was discovering life. I wanted to keep unraveling the layers of joy I was discovering in my work. This led to a desire to expand.

I was breaking out of the imposter syndrome.

Believing that within me was a message worth sharing.

When I started on this path, I was insecure in my voice. I had ideas, passion, and determination, but there was always a voice sowing doubt and uncertainty. It made me question what value I had to offer others or if I was walking the right path. In my head, I always believed myself capable. But, in reality, I was sabotaging my path.

Reacting.

Placing blame on others.

Hiding behind intellect.

I was protecting myself. Afraid to fully step into my power.

In this email, there's so much clarity. There's a confidence not seen before. I'm trusting that I have a gift to offer the world and want to share it.

I see now I was trying to push this expansion. It's in plain sight, in the barrage of questions I throw at Rob.

And he once again reminds me of

"the real truth, the truth behind the truth:
it's not about work.
it's about flow."

I was back to forcing my way instead of flowing. Old habits are hard to break. It's been my default way of living. Attempting to solve problems in my head instead of feeling my way forward or experimenting to see what feels authentic to me.

In my ambition, I'd forgotten what had led me to this point.

If I started looking at this desire as another burden to carry, it was going to remove the joy I was feeling. I would be putting pressure on my work to be what I wanted it to be. That wouldn't be Eucharist living. I'd be demanding something from my work that it might not be able to give.

But if I could remove the expectations and see it all as a gift I freely give, I could let it be what it was. I could drive down a freeway of green lights with no destination other than the next green light ahead of me. This would assure the joy would travel with me. I would be present and free to fully embrace all that was in front of me without thinking I needed to be somewhere else.

It was Rob's comment on how far I'd traveled that served as the inspiration for this book. I gathered all our emails and set off to see for myself how I'd changed from our first conversation. Just as I was starting to hit a writing groove, a small septic backup in our basement grew into a house-wide project that threatened to throw me off course.

You Know What to Do

About a month after starting this book, our septic tank backed up, causing a flood in the basement. Initially, we thought we'd be getting a new bathroom and office. Great. But as the project developed, we found more issues that had to be addressed before rebuilding. What started as a small basement redesign turned into our entire house being flipped upside down.

The damage revealed we'd been living in a house with substantial hidden mold growth behind the walls and throughout the attic and crawlspace. As the mold was being cleaned, we discovered building materials that contained asbestos. All other work had to be stopped until these materials had been professionally removed. This project quickly took on a life of its own, escalating by the day.

Within the first week, we moved our family out of the house because it was too dangerous to live there.

The focus and decluttering I'd begun disappeared. My headspace was being filled. All I wanted to do was write and create, but I was spending hours with contractors, learning more than I ever wanted to know about mold, asbestos, public adjusters, and how the insurance process works.

Want to know the difference between TEM and PCM asbestos tests? I've got you covered.

Need someone to read mold air-sample test results? Look no further.

My life was bearing witness to the time-proven truth that distractions mysteriously appear when you become more serious about your work.

From: **Dave Stradling**
To: Rob Bell
Date: July 20, 2021

Hey Rob!

I'm working away at the book and having a blast with it!

It's taking a bit longer than I was hoping—right after I started, we had a septic overflow which led to the discovery of hidden mold and asbestos throughout our house. So we've been out of our house for four months living with my in-laws, waiting for insurance, while all the work is being done. It's been a disaster! Our whole house is basically torn upside down.

But I'm slowly chipping away and getting closer to having something I am excited to share. Just wanted to give you an update.

Dave

From: **Rob Bell**
To: Dave Stradling
Date: July 20, 2021

oh man, dave, what a mess
we've had our house torn up and we've lived in my
parents' basement and, wow, will you be glad when
this is over . . .
and what a great report on the book
Onwards!

By July, when I emailed Rob, I was starting to fade. I'd hoped we'd be back in the house by the Fourth of July, but we were still a long way from that. Our insurance had put a hold on the work because they saw the size of our bills and had their "Special Investigative Unit" (aka fraud department) look into our insurance claim. I had to give a recorded statement and tour their team through the house, showing all the damage.

Once work resumed, the discoveries didn't end.

A leak in the roof.

Mice nesting in our HVAC system.

A construction defect in the side of the house where animals and water were getting in.

More mold behind walls.

More loans to be taken out.

It was brutal.

With the ever-widening scope of this project and no end in sight, all the progress I'd been making over the previous years was being threatened.

I wanted to give up. Throw it all in. The heaviness of the year was draining the life out of me. The more time I spent overseeing the house, the more apathetic I became about my work. I was in a familiar place of not caring if I ever gave another sermon. I probably would have made a good mold inspector or general contractor. I was getting plenty of experience. I felt I had nothing to offer anyone.

There were moments of despair when I thought about emailing Rob. Let him know what I was going through. How I felt lost and needed advice on how to keep going. But as I would think about writing an email, something inside stopped me. There was a voice telling me that I knew what to do. As Rob so often reminded me, the wisdom I needed was right there inside me.

Don't fight the exhaustion.

Maintain your health and sanity.

Find ways to let yourself rest and recharge.

Give yourself permission to not care for a season.

Let go of what you can't control.

Be present to your family.

Trust that you'll know when you're ready to get back in the game. Don't rush it.

I didn't need anyone's permission. I just listened to that inner wisdom. I didn't resist when my body was communicating how depleted it was. I did my best to care for myself and maintain my sanity. I took extra vacation. Reworked old sermons. I focused on what I could control. I didn't try to do anything more than the basics of what needed to be done. And yes, more gelato to ease the pain.

We finally made it back home on December 30, 2021, just in time for the new year. It was the best feeling! We'd hoped to be home for Christmas Day but, unsurprisingly given the year we'd had, we were hit by COVID for the week of Christmas.

As the calendar flipped from 2021 to 2022, I slowly began feeling that old desire. Soon, it became a growing hunger. There was an ache for what had been. I knew what I was here to do with my life. And nothing was going to stop me from offering that gift to the world.

Onwards I traveled.

Conclusion

"When the student is ready, the teacher will appear."

I love this quote. I've experienced its truth many times, always seeming to come across the right teacher to guide me through the space I found myself in. This is what happened when I met Rob. I was ready for something beyond what I was experiencing, and Rob was that teacher who guided me through these past eight years. Our conversations helped draw out the power and potential I was already living with but hadn't found the ability to trust. Rob helped me discover trust in myself and the Spirit within that was guiding me.

When I tried searching for who had written the student/teacher quote, I discovered there was a second part to it which I'd never heard before. After reading it, I sat stunned, filled with a sense of sadness and empowerment:

"When the student is truly ready, the teacher disappears."

As I read the second half of that quote for the first time, there was an inner knowing. I was entering a new chapter.

While Rob hasn't disappeared out of my life, I no longer feel the need to rely on him as I did when we first started emailing in 2014. I'd discovered the trust Rob had been pointing me toward the entire time. I experienced this when I trusted myself to know how to walk through the disaster of 2021.

In my heart, I knew I was ready.

Reading these emails has brought back so many memories. Stories I'd long forgotten. They also brought up all the old emotions that arose from the situations I was emailing Rob about. Euphoria, despair, and everything in between. I experienced the whole spectrum. No matter where I was, I always knew Rob would be there to encourage me and provide some much-needed perspective to help me keep going. It's been a gift knowing I had a safe harbor to which I could bring my whole self.

What I saw through my journey of emails was me trusting the Spirit more and more to lead me one step at a time. As I did so, I found the permission I so often sought had been inside me the entire time. In no way was this a linear path. It was a slow, meandering journey—like a river continuing to move downstream while looping back and forth on itself. That's how change works. It takes its time and is never rushed.

What does the next chapter look like? I don't know. And that's the exciting part. The only thing for me to do is sit back, float, and let the river lead me where it will. That's the path to the freedom, power, purpose, and joy we all truly desire.

Acknowledgments

Without Rob Bell, this book wouldn't have been possible. It's been an honor having you in my corner, Rob. Thank you for saying yes to a young pastor looking to improve his speaking. Who knew it would lead here?

Publishing a book is not a solo project. I've been fortunate to have an amazing supporting cast around me:

- Ron Martoia, Rob Parker, Dan Haugh, and the many others who have offered wisdom and guidance for the journey.

- Debbie Emmitt for the editing and making sure it all flowed, Justin Lamperski for the original artwork, Megan McCullough for making the pages look good, and Cassady Adams for all those author pictures.

- Anthony Morici, Alison Morici, and Jeff Borkoski who made this book better by reading and commenting on early drafts. They've been a source of support, encouragement, and inspiration from Day One of writing.

- Awaken Westchester Church, this book is our story. You've believed in our vision of what church can be.

Steph, thank you for twelve years of learning to create a life together.

Also by Dave Stradling

25 DAYS. 25 INVITATIONS.

What if you could have more peace in your life?

What about more hope? Or joy? Or love?

This is the promise of Advent. A season meant to inspire peace, hope, love, and joy. But how can we receive these gifts? How can we have more of the good our hearts desire?

This Advent season, *25 Invitations of Christmas* offers twenty-five opportunities to receive these gifts. Each day leading to Christmas is a fresh surprise, a new invitation. Following the model of traditional advent calendars, *25 Invitations of Christmas* walks through the birth stories of Jesus over a twenty-five day period, pausing to show where we are being invited to step into the story.

Along the way, you'll discover how the peace, hope, love, and joy of Christ born into the world 2,000 years ago aren't confined to the past, but are available for us today.

Available Now on Amazon

Sermon Coaching

For fifteen years, I've been writing and giving sermons. Learning to develop this art has been a joy, and I keep discovering new ways of crafting messages and communicating ideas. If you find yourself stuck somewhere in this process—wondering where to start, what to talk about, how to put a message together, or how to communicate it effectively—I'd love to help.

Whether individually or with a group, I want to help draw out the wisdom you carry within so you can offer the best of yourself to the people and groups you speak to.

Sign up: davestradling.com

About the Author

Dave Stradling is the founder and lead pastor of Awaken Westchester Church. He is the author of *25 Invitations of Christmas: An Advent Devotional.* Dave holds an MDiv from Alliance Theological Seminary and a BA in Christian Thought from Grove City College.

In 2023, his weekly sermon podcast was awarded Best of Westchester and highlighted as one of the top local podcasts in Westchester County, New York, where he lives with his wife and kids.

Stay in Touch

davestradling.com

Instagram: @dave_stradling

Sign-up for weekly emails full of inspiration, my latest thoughts, and updates about my work: davestradling.substack.com

Milton Keynes UK
Ingram Content Group UK Ltd.
UKHW011311250624
444725UK00022B/251